F. Scott Fitzge.

The Great Gatsby

Adapted for the stage by Stephen Sharkey

Bloomsbury Methuen Drama
An imprint of Bloomsbury Publishing Plc

B L O O M S B U R Y
LONDON · OXFORD · NEW YORK · NEW DELHI · SYDNEY

Bloomsbury Methuen Drama
An imprint of Bloomsbury Publishing Plc

Imprint previously known as Methuen Drama

50 Bedford Square	1385 Broadway
London	New York
WC1B 3DP	NY 10018
UK	USA

www.bloomsbury.com

Bloomsbury is a registered trade mark of Bloomsbury Publishing Plc

First published 2015

© Stephen Sharkey, 2015

British Library Cataloguing-in-Publication Data
A catalogue record for this book is available from the British Library.

ISBN: PB: 978-1-4742-7511-8
ePub: 978-1-4742-7512-5
ePDF: 978-1-4742-7513-2

Library of Congress Cataloging-in-Publication Data
A catalog record for this book is available from the Library of Congress.

Typeset by Mark Heslington Ltd, Scarborough, North Yorkshire
Printed and bound in Great Britain

The Great Gatsby

This adaptation of *The Great Gatsby* was first produced by Blackeyed Theatre at Devonshire Park Theatre, Eastbourne, on 8 September 2015 with the following cast:

Nick Carraway	Adam Jowett
Tom Buchanan	Tristan Pate
Daisy Buchanan	Celia Cruwys-Finnigan
Jordan Baker	Celeste De Veazey
George Wilson	Tom Neill
Myrtle Wilson	Stacey Ghent
Jay Gatsby	Max Roll

All other parts played by members of the company

Director	Eliot Giuralarocca
Musical Director and Arranger	Ellie Verkerk
Designer	Victoria Spearing
Movement Director	Bronya Deutsch
Lighting Designer	Charlotte McClelland
Costume Designer	Jenny Little
Projection Designer	Stephen Harrison
Producer	Adrian McDougall

BLACKEYED
THEATRE

Blackeyed Theatre has been creating exciting, sustainable theatre throughout the UK since 2004. We have taken our work to over a hundred different theatres across England, Scotland and Wales, from 50 seat studios to 1,000 seat opera houses.

Central to everything we do is our desire both to challenge and engage artists and audiences. As a company that receives minimal funding, we are proof that commercially successful theatre can still be innovative and can still surprise. We believe that only by balancing a desire to push artistic boundaries with an appreciation of what audiences have a desire to see do you create theatre that is truly sustainable, both commercially and artistically.

We bring together artists with a genuine passion for the work they produce, offering a theatrical experience that's both artistically excellent and affordable.

Our previous national tours include *Not About Heroes* (Stephen MacDonald), *Dracula* (Bram Stoker, adapted by John Ginman), *Teechers* (John Godber), *Mother Courage and Her Children* (Bertolt Brecht), *The Trial* (Steven Berkoff), *The Caucasian Chalk Circle* (Bertolt Brecht), *Alfie* (Bill Naughton), *The Cherry Orchard* (Anton Chekhov), *Oh What a Lovely War* (Joan Littlewood), the world première of *Oedipus* (Steven Berkoff) and *The Resistible Rise of Arturo Ui* (Bertolt Brecht).

In 2011, Blackeyed Theatre launched Pulse, a new-writing competition. The winning script, *The Beekeeper* by Michael Ashton, enjoyed a three-week London Fringe run, receiving three OFFIE nominations, including Best New Play.

The company is resident at South Hill Park Arts Centre in Bracknell, where we continue to create accessible theatre that challenges expectations, furthering our reputation as one of the UK's leading touring theatre companies.

"One of the most innovative, audacious companies working in contemporary English theatre"
The Stage

www.blackeyedtheatre.co.uk

The Great Gatsby
By F. Scott Fitzgerald
Adapted by Stephen Sharkey

**Produced by Blackeyed Theatre
in association with South Hill Park Arts Centre and
Eastbourne Theatres**

Cast

Nick Carraway	Adam Jowett
Tom Buchanan	Tristan Pate
Daisy Buchanan	Celia Cruwys-Finnigan
Jordan Baker	Celeste De Veazey
George Wilson	Tom Neill
Myrtle Wilson	Stacey Ghent
Jay Gatsby	Max Roll

All other parts played by members of the cast

Creative Team

Writer	Stephen Sharkey
Director	Eliot Giuralarocca
Musical Director	Ellie Verkerk
Designer	Victoria Spearing
Movement Director	Bronya Deutsch
Lighting Designer	Charlotte McClelland
Costume Designer	Jenny Little
Projection Designer	Stephen Harrison
Education Advisor	Danielle Corbishley
Press Relations	Chloe Nelkin Consulting
Education Pack	Shelley Upton
Properties	Chantal Addley
Set Contruction	Russell Pearn and Steve Spearing
Producer	Adrian McDougall

With thanks to Ron McAllister, Chris Jordan, Rebecca Wire, Shana Rodrigues, Sally Little, Bronwyn Hodgkins, East Berkshire Operatic Society and Katy Lethbridge.

Blackeyed Theatre is proud to be supporting Ataxia UK through this production.

Cast

Adam Jowett | Nick Carraway

Adam graduated in 2009 from The Arden School of Theatre. Since then he has gone on to co-create a number of award winning short films, plays and sketch shows with his Manchester based company, *Blackhand Productions.*

Theatre credits include Claudio in *Much Ado About Nothing,* Cassio in *Othello* (Demi-Paradise Productions/Lancaster Castle), Macduff in *Macbeth* (Courtyard Theatre, London) and Ross in *Macbeth* (Oldham Coliseum).

Television credits include *Scott & Bailey, Last Tango In Halifax* (Red Production Company), *Shameless* (Company Pictures) and *Emmerdale* (ITV). Adam is also a self taught drummer and guitarist.

Tristan Pate | Tom Buchanan

Tristan trained at the Birmingham School of Acting.

Theatre credits include *Dusty* (Charing Cross Theatre), *The Comedy of Errors* and *Wuthering Heights* (Red Rose Chain), *The Institute of Impossibility* (Belgrade Theatre), *Cider With Rosie* (Everyman Theatre, Cheltenham and UK tour), *Dreamboats and Petticoats* (UK tour and West End), *Mother Courage* (Blackeyed Theatre, UK tour), *Anna Karenina* (Arcola Theatre), *Black Beauty* (UK tour), *I, Bertolt Brecht* (UK tour), *Snow White* (South Hill Park) and *Jack and the Beanstalk* (The Mill Arts Centre).

Tristan is delighted to return to Blackeyed Theatre after appearing in their production of *Mother Courage and Her Children* in 2012. He would like to thank his fiancée and daughter for their continued support. www.tristanpate.co.uk

Celia Cruwys-Finnigan | Daisy Buchanan

Celia graduated from Rose Bruford in 2015.

Her theatre credits include Gretchen in *The Bureau of Lost Things* (Theatre 503), while her television work includes Mo in *The Walkers* (SKY 1).

Her theatre work while training includes Lily in *Punk Rock*, Annie in *All My Sons*, Maggie in *Cat On A Hot Tin Roof*, Lady Anne in *Richard III*, Thaliard/Leonine in *Pericles*, Elizabeth Bradley in *Today,* Woman 1 in *Songs For A New World*, Liz in *The Wall*.

Celeste De Veazey | Jordan Baker

Celeste is a recent graduate of the Actor Musicianship course at Rose Bruford College. She made her professional debut as an actor-musician at the age of 15 in *A Little Night Music* at the Chatelet Theatre in Paris.

Her credits also include Katja in *The Bureau of Lost Things* (Theatre503) and Ghost/fortune teller in *The EA Sims 4* game soundtrack. Her theatre work whilst training includes Cissy in *Punk Rock*, Lady Macbeth in *Macbeth*, Rosalind in *As You Like It*, Karelia in *Summerfolk* and Woman 1 in *Songs for a New World*, and Joyce in radio play *The Wall*.

Celeste has always been drawn towards the roaring 20s so is thrilled to be part of Gatsby and have the honour of working with Blackeyed Theatre.

Tom Neill | George Wilson

Tom grew up in Berkshire, taking drama and music lessons and performing with community groups. He trained in Music with Theatre Studies at Huddersfield University.

He has a long association with Blackeyed Theatre and previous acting credits with the company include the UK tours of *The Cherry Orchard, The Resistible Rise of Arturo Ui* and *Oh What A Lovely War,* the latter affording the additional reward of meeting with Brian Murphy, one of the cast of Joan Littlewood's original show.

Other theatre work includes the no.1 tour of Britten's *Death in Venice* in a beautiful setting by Yoshi Oida (Opera North), pioneering site-specific works *Don't Look Back* at Somerset House (dreamthinkspeak) and *1000 Revolutions Per Moment (Periplum)*. He has toured to primary, secondary and special educational needs schools, and last Christmas around care homes (for Tickled Pink) as well as playing in pantomime for several companies.

Tom is also a theatre director, musician, composer and script writer, recently adapting the stage première of James Joyce's *A Portrait of the Artist as a Young Man* (Pentameters), composing *The Refuge* (for Beautiful Creatures) and recording *More Than You Can Eat*, the debut album of folk-soul-jazz collective *The Herberts*.

Tom lives in Bracknell where he volunteers for the local Labour Party. He currently supports the campaign for global access to clean water by donating a tenth of his income to Wateraid UK. www.tomneill.co.uk

Stacey Ghent | Myrtle Wilson

Stacey was born in South Shields, Tyne and Wear, and graduated from the American Musical Theatre Academy of London (AMTA) in July 2013. Since then she has also trained with the Actors Class and the Acting Network.

Her theatre credits include Nellie/ Actor-Musician in *The Threepenny Opera* (UK tour), Actor-Musician in *Raymond Briggs' Father Christmas* (Lyric Hammersmith) Janine in *Reasons to be Cheerful, The Festival* (UK & Germany), Connie in *Passport to Pimlico: Rehearsed Reading* (SouthWestFest), and Actor-Musician in *The Opinion Makers* (Mercury Theatre and Derby Theatre).

As a vocalist her credits include *Naked Noise: Neil John Onions, Sondheim: Women, Hannah Waddingham and Her Band, Julie Atherton: All I Want For Christmas is an Audience, Julie Atherton & Laura Pitt-Pullford: Partners in Crime* (all St James Theatre), *Christmas in New York* (Palace Theatre, London) and *Julie Atherton: Rush of Life* (album launch).

Television credits include Nurse Morris in *Breathless* (ITV).

Stacey is also very proud to be a member of The Daisy Chains, an all-female 1950s rock and roll band (www. thedaisychains.co.uk).

She has recently filmed *Shrink: Season 1*, a new web series due to air in the autumn of 2015 (www.facebook.com/ ShrinkTV). www.staceylghent.com

Max Roll | Jay Gatsby

Max graduated from the Yale School of Drama in 2013.

Since then he has worked both in the United States and the UK. His recent stage work includes Benedick in *Much Ado About Nothing* for RBL Theatre and Nick in the US regional premier of A.R. Gurney's *Family Furniture*. He also continues to workshop and develop *Redrum: A Musical Parody of The Shining*.

Credits at Yale include title roles in Shakespeare's *King Lear* and *Antony and Cleopatra*, as well as *The Seagull*, *Angels in America* and several new plays.

Max has also lent his voice to video games and audio books including Stefanie Zweig's Oscar winning *Nowhere in Africa* and the sequel, *Somewhere in Germany*.

Stephen Sharkey | Writer

Stephen's writing for the stage includes *Sex and the Three Day Week* (Liverpool Playhouse), *The Glass Slipper* (Northern Stage, Newcastle), *The Resistible Rise of Arturo Ui* (Liverpool Playhouse/Nottingham Playhouse), *Peter Pan* (Northern Stage), *Cloudcuckooland* (Pleasance Theatre, London and Edinburgh, and UK tour), *Hansel and Gretel* (Northern Stage), *The Yellow Wallpaper* (Royal Festival Hall), *The May Queen* (Liverpool Everyman), *A Christmas Carol* (Northern Stage), *Ion* (Gate Theatre, Notting Hill), *The Old Curiosity Shop* (Southwark Playhouse), *Oblomov* (Pleasance, London and Edinburgh), *The Gambler* (Pleasance, Edinburgh).

His forthcoming projects include *Inkheart* (with Walter Meierjohann, Home, Manchester), while for BBC Radio his work includes *The Visitation*, *Kepler's Mum's a Witch*, *All of You on the Good Earth* (winner of the Society of Authors' prize for best radio debut).

Eliot Giuralarocca | Director

Eliot studied English Language and Literature at Christ Church, Oxford before training at the Guildford School of Acting.

Directing credits include national tours of *Not About Heroes* and *Dracula* for Blackeyed Theatre, *The Imperfect Pearl* (Whitehouse Productions), *West Side Story* (Belgrade Theatre/Armonico Consort), *Baroque Around the Block* and *Monteverdi's Flying Circus* (Armonico Consort), *Knackerman* (White Bear Theatre), *Three Servants* and *Voyagers* (Jet Theatre/Croydon Warehouse) and *The Love Letters of Private Blade* (Riverside Studios).

Work as an actor includes *The Beekeeper* (Blackeyed Theatre, OFFIE nominated for Best Actor), *Alarms and Excursions* (Chipping Norton), *The Resistible Rise of Arturo Ui* (Liverpool Playhouse/Nottingham Playhouse), *Il Turco in*

Italia (Royal Opera House), *Measure for Measure* (Thelma Holt Productions), *A Small Family Business* (Watford Palace Theatre), *Don't Look Now* (Sheffield Theatres/Lyric Hammersmith), *The Comedy of Errors* and *Titus Andronicus* (Shakespeare's Globe), *Twelfth Night* (Royal Exchange Manchester), *Rosencrantz and Guildenstern are Dead* and *Horse and Carriage* (West Yorkshire Playhouse), *A Midsummer Night's Dream* and *The Tempest* (Nuffield Theatre Southampton) and *The Government Inspector* (Salisbury Playhouse).

Ellie Verkerk | Musical Director and Arranger

Ellie graduated from the Royal College of Music as a pianist, accompanist and orchestral musician, and has worked with a broad variety of musicians, singers and singer-songwriters, from London's West End to recording sessions, cabarets, weddings and beyond.

She was the assistant to the conductor and production assistant to the film director for *Celebrating John Lord* (Royal Albert Hall) and has worked as a keys player for *Jersey Boys* (Prince Edward Theatre). Her work as Musical Director includes *Beauty and the Beast, Oh What A Lovely War, Mother Courage* and *Dracula* (Blackeyed Theatre), and various cabarets for South Hill Park. Her work as Assistant Musical Director includes *Kerrigan-Lowdermilk LIVE* (St James Theatre), and *All I Want for Christmas …* (Julie Atherton, St James Theatre). Recording and session work includes *My Parade (*Stephanie Fearon), and singer-songwriters Dear Pariah and Buswell. She has appeared as a trumpet player in music videos, and conducted a symphony orchestra at the Shepherd's Bush Empire as part of the *Underground Orchestra Challenge* with Sean Buswell.

Ellie is a passionate supporter of young people, teaching and supporting those who aspire to work professionally in the creative arts industry, and works at the Read Dance and

Theatre College (Reading, Berkshire). In addition to her musical work, Ellie is also a massage therapist, specialising in the treatment of musicians and performers, and works regularly with people with special needs. www.EllieVerkerk.com

Victoria Spearing | Designer

Graduating from Bretton Hall in Theatre Design and Technology in 2001, Victoria started work as a freelance set designer with South Hill Park Arts Centre, where she is now resident designer.

This will be the twentieth design for Blackeyed Theatre, from *The Caretaker* to the highly acclaimed tours of *Not About Heroes*, *Dracula* and *Teechers*. Her design for *The Beekeeper* was nominated for the Best Set Design in the 2012 Off West End Theatre Awards.

She has designed over 100 sets for a variety of companies, producing initial sketches and model boxes through to involvement in set building, painting and final dressing.

For South Hill Park she has designed the last twelve pantomimes, as well as a range of in-house productions, including *Summer Holiday*, *Brassed Off*, *Stepping Out*, *Blood Brothers*, *Calendar Girls*, *Oliver!*, *Henry V*, *The Tempest*, *Billy Elliot* and *Oh What A Lovely War*. She also redesigned South Hill Park's Wilde Theatre Bar and Foyer to create a new performance space.

Her design work for other companies includes the world première of *A Little History of the World* (Watermill Theatre), *The Dumb Waiter*, *Miss Julie*, *Waiting for Godot*, *Race* and *The Nativity That Goes Wrong* (Reading Rep), *Journey's End*, *Dancing at Lughnasa*, *The Madness of George III*, *Three Men in a Boat* and *Birdsong* (Original Theatre Company), *Lotty's War* (Giddy Ox), *Loserville* (Youth Music Theatre), *The History Boys* and *Danny the Champion of the World* (London Contemporary Theatre), as well as various Christmas shows for The Castle, Wellingborough.

She lives in a small village with her husband and daughter and is currently using her design skills to transform her garden, that is of course when she is not busy reading a script, crafting a detailed model box or splattered with paint.

Bronya Deutsch | Movement Director

Bronya is a movement director, actor and theatre maker based in the UK. She trained at Mountview Academy of Theatre Arts as an actor and at École Jacques Lecoq, graduating in 2014.

As a movement director she has most recently worked with Ian Forrest at Theatre by the Lake, Keswick on their touring production of *Two* and also with John Terry at The Theatre, Chipping Norton (*Around the World in Eighty Days* and *My Mother Said I Never Should*). She has also worked as mask consultant on *The Emperor Jones* for Lost Theatre.

She performs internationally as a clown and an actor, and works regularly with the Flying Seagull Project circus and physical theatre ensemble, Wet Picnic.

Charlotte McClelland | Lighting Designer

Charlotte trained on an Arts Council bursary at Central School of Speech and Drama.

Previous work for Blackeyed Theatre includes *Art, The Resistible Rise of Arturo Ui, Oedipus, Oh What A Lovely War, The Trial, The Beekeeper, Dracula, Not About Heroes* and *Teechers*.

Other recent lighting designs include *The Photophonic Experiment* for Contemporary Music Network, *Angels on High* for Guildford International Music Festival (vertical dance on Guildford Cathedral), *Carmen* and *The Marriage of Figaro* for Longborough Festival Opera, *Snow White* for South Hill Park Arts Centre, *The Baghdad Monologue, Lamentations* and *Chicos del 21* for Frances M Lynch/ Electric Voice Theatre.

Jenny Little | Costume Designer

Jenny graduated with a BA (Hons) in Costume for the Screen and Stage from the Arts Institute at Bournemouth.

Costume designs for previous Blackeyed Theatre productions include *Mother Courage and Her Children, Dracula, Not About Heroes* and *Teechers*.

Other credits include *West Side Story* for the Armonico Consort (Belgrade Coventry), several pantomimes for Evolution Productions, *The Lands, Dancing on the Waves, Fiesta Latina Nights, Jazz a la Carte* and *Studio 54* for American company Jean Ann Ryan Productions, as well as *Virus* for Bournemouth Direct Theatre School. Jenny has also worked on textile production for West End shows including *The Lion King, Oliver!* and *Wicked*, and as Wardrobe Assistant on *Les Miserables* at the Queen's Theatre. When Jenny is not working in theatre she works freelance designing and making bespoke costumes and special occasion garments for individuals.

Stephen Harrison | Projection Designer

Stephen is a digital creative practitioner specialising in projection and lighting design, filmmaking, photography and live streaming. He studied Software Engineering at the University of Sheffield and worked in the IT industry before moving full-time into the performing arts.

Previous projection designs include *Good To Be Bad, Ghost Station* and *Oliver!* (Artemis Studios). Lighting credits include *Thoroughly Modern Millie, Our Country's Good, Frankenstein, Good To Be Bad, Ghost Station, Oliver, Henry's Arabian Nights, Norfolk's Rose* and *Christmas Carol*.

As producer for SHPLive, an Arts Council funded live streaming programme, Stephen worked on the design and implementation of several ground-breaking tramsmedia productions, including *Mars One Extended* and *The Lamellar Project*. He will also be producing Lightwork's *Hecabe* for the Fast Forward Festival in Athens in 2016.

Additionally, Stephen works as a Company Stage Manager, with recent touring credits including *Dracula, Teechers* and *Beauty and The Beast* (Blackeyed Theatre), *Lotty's War, Rebel Cell* and *Beautiful Thing* (Giddy Ox Theatre) and *Frankenstein* (Proteus Theatre). www.stephenharrison.me.uk

Danielle Corbishley | Education Advisor

Danielle trained at Dartington and gained a PGCert in Physical Theatre with Jasmin Vardimon Company. She is a performer, director, lecturer and magician who develops and directs performances with Beautiful Creatures Theatre alongside her education and freelance theatre work.

Beautiful Creatures produces physical and visual theatre for audiences of all ages throughout the UK and curates a programme of outdoor arts at Caversham Festival, providing opportunities for young people to gain vocational experience.

Danielle is currently touring with Periplum's *451* as Company Stage Manager and Performer. Her previous education work for Blackeyed Theatre includes *Mother Courage and Her Children, Dracula, Not About Heroes* and *Teechers*. www.beautifulcreatures.org.uk

Adrian McDougall | Producer

Adrian is the founder and Artistic Director of Blackeyed Theatre. He grew up in Berkshire, studying modern languages at Southampton University, going on to work in marketing and PR, before establishing Blackeyed Theatre in 2004.

Since Blackeyed Theatre's very first production, *Effie's Burning*, he has produced nineteen national tours, including the world premiere of Steven Berkoff's *Oedipus* and a brand new stage adaptation of Bram Stoker's *Dracula*. As a director, his credits include – for Blackeyed Theatre – the world première of *The Beekeeper* and national tours of *Oh What A Lovely War, Teechers* and *Alfie*, as well as *Brassed*

Off and *House and Garden* (for South Hill Park). He has also worked as an actor, touring the UK with Oddsocks Productions, Premier Stage Productions and the Phoenix Theatre Company.

Adrian is also a director of CentreStage Partnership, a leading provider of experiential learning and behavioural coaching to organisations from the public and private sectors (www.cstage.co.uk). He lives in Bracknell with his wife and daughter, supporting and participating in community theatre when he can.

Chloé Nelkin Consulting | Press Relations

Chloé Nelkin Consulting was founded in 2010 and specialises in PR, events and consultancy with a dedicated focus on theatre, visual arts and opera. With a passion for the arts and communicating the importance of culture to today's society, CNC is a small, dynamic company that always delivers with style and sophistication. The company handles multiple sell-out productions of all sizes across all genres of theatre. Some recent theatre work includes: *As Is* (Trafalgar Studios), *The Ted Bundy Project* by Greg Wohead (UK tour), *A Simple Space* (Udderbelly), *No Milk for the Foxes* (Camden People's Theatre), *Dead Royal* by Chris Ioan Roberts (Ovalhouse), *Product* by Mark Ravenhill (Arcola Theatre), *Hiraeth* (Soho Theatre), *Lardo* (Old Red Lion), *Ablutions* (Soho Theatre), *WINK* by Phoebe Eclair-Powell (Theatre503), *Blind Man's Song* (UK tour), *The Diary of a Nobody* (King's Head Theatre), *Miss Havisham's Expectations* (Trafalgar Studios) and *Damn Yankees* (Landor Theatre). www.chloenelkinconsulting.com.

South Hill Park Arts Centre

South Hill Park Arts Centre has been providing a huge range of arts experiences in East Berkshire for over forty years.

Over the past twelve years South Hill Park has been actively involved in touring work all over the UK with its associate companies Original Theatre, Icarus Theatre Collective, and its resident company Blackeyed Theatre company. This has allowed the work of the arts centre, and the creative teams it has sought to develop, to reach more than eighty venues from the North of Scotland down to Cornwall, also taking in Ireland and Wales on some tours. Most of these productions are designed and built right here at South Hill Park, helping to develop the centre's fast growing reputation as the creative heart of Berkshire.

Over the last two years, South Hill Park has also been working closely with its new associate companies Squint, HookHitch, London Contemporary Theatre and Theatre Re, proudly presenting their previews en route to the Edinburgh Festival Fringe.

South Hill Park is particularly proud to have collaborated with Blackeyed Theatre on some of the most extraordinary actor/musician productions to have toured the UK from 2007 to the present and is looking forward to doing so again for many years to come. The arts are all about partnerships and South Hill Park is fortunate to have Blackeyed Theatre as a partner.

www.southhillpark.org.uk

Eastbourne Theatres

Eastbourne Theatres is currently the only local authority owned theatre in the country not only producing work in-house but also touring its productions.

Eastbourne Theatres began producing in 2001 with Alan Ayckbourn's *Relatively Speaking*. Subsequent productions include: *Barnum*, *Nunsense*, *Neville's Island*, *By Jeeves*, *Funny Money*, *Taking Steps*, *Stepping Out*, *Gotta Sing Gotta Dance*, *Last of the Summer Wine*, *Murder By Misadventure*, *Private Lives* many of which have toured nationally. Since 2001 they have also been producing the famous *Devonshire Park Pantomime* in-house.

As co-producers Eastbourne Theatres have worked with New Vic Productions on shows including *Telstar* (tour and West End), *The Quiz* starring David Bradley (tour and West End), national tours of *Blonde Poison*, *Miss Dietrich Regrets* and *Swimming at the Ritz* as well as seasons of new work including several world premiere productions.

Other collaborators include Original Theatre Company with *The Madness of George III*, *Twelfth Night* and *See How They Run*.

Eastbourne Theatres have even co-produced an Ice Show with sixteen international ice skaters and a cast of West End singers!

www.eastbournetheatres.co.uk

Ataxia UK

Ataxia is an umbrella term given to a group of neurological conditions that can affect balance, coordination and speech. Ataxia affects around 10,000 people in the UK and as a charity, Ataxia UK works on behalf of the people affected by the condition. We receive no government funding and therefore the generous gifts from our dedicated fundraisers go a long way.

The provision of healthcare for those with ataxia has improved considerably over the past fifty years, however there is still a great deal of work to be done. Ultimately our vision at Ataxia UK is a world free of ataxia, therefore a significant part of the funds raised go directly to promoting research, with the aim of finding treatments and a cure for ataxia by 2020. The charity also operates a dedicated helpline and a network of branches and support groups, as well as running awareness campaigns and fundraising activities.

www.ataxia.org.uk

In conversation with Stephen Sharkey

Can you tell us more about your background and your journey to becoming a playwright?

I was a grammar school boy from a working class family in Liverpool, and went from there to read Classics at Oxford, where I started writing plays. My first script was an adaptation of Oscar Wilde's *The Picture of Dorian Gray*. When we took it to the Edinburgh Fringe Al 'The Pub Landlord' Murray went on one night as the butler. Since then I've written adaptations of Greek tragedy, French farce, Russian satire and English classics like *The Old Curiosity Shop*.

What was it that enticed you to take on *The Great Gatsby*?

Fitzgerald's novel is a masterpiece of storytelling and written in such cool, elegant prose, it sparkles and seduces like the champagne in bowls at Gatsby's parties. For me as a playwright, the opportunity to immerse myself in a work of this quality and try to realise it for the stage was far too good to miss. Funnily enough, the experience of adapting *Gatsby* took me back to *The Picture of Dorian Gray,* all those years ago. The stories have themes in common: class and morality, appearance and reality, time and mortality. But they also feature absolutely priceless dialogue, begging to be spoken aloud.

What were the key challenges with the adaptation?

It's quite a challenge for an adaptor to take on, as you need to find a way to convey the driving, forward momentum of the tragedy while allowing the characters to live in the moment, and giving us time to observe them in the rarified air of that particular place and time, the 'jazz age'. Blackeyed Theatre were always keen from the beginning that this production would have a strong musical element, and this was a brilliant instinct: the music and songs help enormously in evoking the atmosphere, the world of the novel, and they also helped me in composing a structural rhythm for the script. One of my writing heroes is the late, great Dennis Potter whose miraculous use of popular music in his plays had a huge influence on a generation of playwrights. Great writers like Potter, Fitzgerald, and Dickens before them, knew the high dramatic value of a cheap song.

What parallels can be drawn between the 1920s world of Jay Gatsby and the apparent class/wealth divide of today?

Fitzgerald wrestled with the title for his novel and it was almost published as *Trimalchio in West Egg*. Trimalchio is a character in the Roman work *Satyricon*, a freed slave who has acquired fantastical, spectacular wealth through hard work and opportunism; Fitzgerald looked back 2,000 years to see a parallel in ancient Rome for the epic self-made luxury of Gatsby's mansion. The tycoon, and tales of his fortunes and misfortunes, is a constant in human history and in fiction, from Aladdin to Abramovitch, Trimalchio to Gatsby, King Midas to Bill Gates. The vast majority of us only ever know these people through myth, and we are fascinated by them. Fitzgerald was drawn to them, certainly, but his genius was to crystallise and dramatise the tragedy of one such mythical tycoon and make his a story for all time.

What do you hope audiences will get from this adaptation?

I can only hope that people enjoy the play and the characters, and that those who know the novel will like the immediacy and verve of the production and perhaps find something new to think about. I hope that those who don't know the novel will seek it out and read it, and think favourably of my adaptation when they do so.

A note from the Adaptor

It hardly seems appropriate for the adaptor of such an exquisitely bejewelled masterpiece as *The Great Gatsby* to presume to say anything here in the way of analysis or even introduction. Far sharper and better qualified people have spilled lakes of ink in the criticism, interpretation and appreciation of the novel. Among these, I recommend you seek out Sarah Churchwell's riveting and beautifully written *Careless People: Murder, Mayhem and the Invention of The Great Gatsby*, a brilliant piece of literary detective work. For myself, I only hope that in shaping the story for the stage I have managed to capture something of the beauty and force, rhythm and sensuality of the original.

Fitzgerald's ambition for his novel was striking: he said he wanted to write something 'better than I am capable of'. There's a playful self-deprecation in this, as he was rightly proud of his skill as a prose artist and storyteller: even when critics were at their most strident he held that essential kernel of self-belief. But importantly 'Fitz' was also reaching, like Gatsby, for some species of perfection. Of course his great story, and his greatest character, are all about the money. And as Sarah Churchwell points out with typical acuity, 'consumption is very conspicuous indeed in *Gatsby*, a catalogue of possessions from Gatsby's spectacular Rolls-Royce to Daisy's $350,000 string of pearls ... They called such items "goods" for a reason: purchasing was acquiring a moral valence.' Money and morals, goods and goodness: these are Fitzgerald's themes, or a large plank of them, at any rate. Love, sex and marriage, the pursuit of pleasure, the iniquities of class in a capitalist economy ... but there I go, introducing. I should leave that to the experts. As far the play is concerned, I had an ambition of my own, or rather a challenge, issued to me by fellow playwright Meredydd Barker: not to mess up his favourite novel. Except he used a different four-letter word.

Many thanks to Adrian McDougall of Blackeyed Theatre for the commission and all his hard work on the production.

To Eliot Giuralarocca for careful and creative script advice and direction. To Nick Cavaliere, Claire Empson, Robin Kingsland and Mayou Trikerioti for their help. This play is dedicated, once again, to Rebecca.

Stephen Sharkey

The Great Gatsby

Characters

Nick Carraway
Daisy Buchanan, *Nick's cousin*
Tom Buchanan, *Daisy's husband*
Jordan Baker, *a professional golfer*
George Wilson, *a garage owner*
Myrtle Wilson, *George's wife*
Jay Gatsby

Other parts played by the company:

Chester McKee, *a musician*
Catherine, *Myrtle's sister*
Meyer Wolfshiem, *a gangster*
James C. Gatz, *Gatsby's father*
Partygoers: Sarah, Owl-Eyes, Treves, Klipspringer, Ross, Miss Baedeker
Servant, Butler

New York City and Long Island, 1922.

A note about music

Fitzgerald mentions four contemporary songs by name in the novel, deploying them with subtlety and irony and to great effect: *The Sheik of Araby, Ain't We Got Fun?, Three O'Clock in the Morning,* and *The Love Nest.* This production also makes use of these, supplemented by music from other classic songs of the period such as: *Who's Sorry Now?, Baby Won't You Please Come Home, April Showers, Somebody Stole My Gal,* and *The Rosary.*

Overture

Gatsby's mansion, after midnight.

The company play and sing and dance. They come to a raucous conclusion and then speak as a chorus, swapping lines, talking to each other and to us.

Chorus   Summer nights
Out on Long Island
Summer of '22
We accept his hospitality –
Gatsby's –
Paying him the subtle tribute
Of knowing nothing whatever about him.
From East Egg come the Chester Beckers
And the Leeches
And a man named Bunsen, whom I knew at Yale
And Doctor Webster Civet
Who will drown a few summers later, up at Maine
And the Hornbeams
And a whole clan named Buckbeak
Who flip their noses like goats at you if you come near.
Also from East Egg come the Chrysties
And Edgar Beaver, and Clarence Endive –
Didn't he fight with you in the garden?
He's a bum! –
Would you reach me a rose, honey?
Pour me a drop in that there crystal glass.
From farther out on the Island come the Cheadles
The O.R.P. Schraders
The Stonewall Jackson Abrams
And Ripley Snell was here three days before he went to the penitentiary
Yes, and so drunk out on the gravel drive
Oh God!
An automobile ran over his right hand.
Who else?
The Dancies of course

The Hammerheads
And Beluga the tobacco importer
With all his girls
Not forgetting
Who ever could?
And from West Egg, across the bay?
East Egg, West Egg, what's the difference?
East is old money, my dear
And West is the new stuff –
Cecil Roebuck, Cecil Bernstein
Newton Orchid, from MGM
Clyde Cohen, Don Schwartze
Fellows all connected with the movies in one way or another.
Senator Gulick
The Catlips, the Bembergs
The promoter, Da Fontano, who comes to gamble
With Ed LeGros, and James B. Ferret
'Rot-Gut' to his many customers
And when Ferret wanders into the garden under the star-peppered sky
You know he was cleaned out.
A man named Klipspringer is here so often we call him 'The Boarder' –
I doubt he has any other home –
Theatrical people.
Broadway people.
Showgirls and sports people.
From New York they come, in fleets of cars
The Chromes, the Dennickers
The Corrigans, the Scullys
The young Mr and Mrs Quinn –
Soon divorced –
All these people are at Gatsby's house in the summer
And not one was actually invited.
Oh, none of us was invited
Were you?
No!

Nick   Pardon me? – but I was invited.

Chorus   You were?

Bully for you.

And who might you be?

Nick   Nick Carraway, how do you do. I live in the cottage over the way –

Chorus   You do?

That eyesore!

Well, I like it!

Nick   As do I.

Chorus   You say Gatsby invited you?

Say, this fella was invited!

He's Gatsby's neighbour!

Is he really the Kaiser's nephew?

I heard he was a spy.

Nick   I'm afraid I don't know. I haven't met him.

Chorus   Well of course you haven't.

What line are you in?

The movies?

A musician?

Nick   Me? No. No – I'm in bonds.

Chorus   Bonds?

Nick   Securities, investments – I'm learning the ropes, still, there's an awful lot of studying, mountains of it as a matter of fact –

Chorus (*cutting him off*)   My God – is that Gilda Gray?
Where?
Out on the canvas
You don't say!

That's not Gilda Gray
From the *Follies*?
That's her understudy
Had me fooled!
She's too exquisite, whoever she is!
Let's take a closer look
Yes!
Excuse us!

They leave.

Nick   You are excused . . .

Quite by accident I had rented a house in one of the strangest communities in North America.

By summer's end I'd given up on New York and on Wall Street, left the whole sad circus behind and returned home to the Mid West. I wanted the world to be in uniform and at a sort of moral attention forever. I'd had my fill of riotous excursions and privileged glimpses into the human heart. Matter of fact – I hated this whole damn crowd.

Only Gatsby was exempt. For there was something . . . gorgeous about him, an extraordinary gift for hope, a romantic readiness such as I have never found in any other person. No – Gatsby turned out all right at the end. Those who preyed on the man, and the foul dust that floated in the wake of his dreams – they are what truly disgust me.

I suppose it all began the night I drove around the bay to East Egg, to have dinner with the Buchanans – Daisy, my second cousin, and Tom, whom I knew at Yale.

Scene One

Daisy and **Jordan** *are reclining, fanning themselves gently. It's hot.* **Tom** *brings* **Nick** *a drink.*

Tom   I've got a nice place here. Belonged to Demaine, the oil man. We'll go inside.

They turn and approach the women. **Daisy** *tries to stir.*

Nick   Daisy.

Daisy   I'm paralyzed with happiness!

Nick   Don't get up on my account.

Daisy   You're so *good*. This is my friend, Miss Baker.

Jordan   Hello.

Nick   How do you do.

Daisy   You were in Chicago, Nick?

Nick   Only a day.

Daisy   How is everybody? Do they miss me?

Nick   The whole town is desolate. All the cars have the left rear wheel painted black, as a mark of respect.

Daisy   How marvellous! Let's go back, Tom. Tomorrow! You ought to see the baby girl.

Nick   I'd love to.

Daisy   She's sleeping right now. You ought to see her, though, she's –

Tom   What you doing these days, Nick?

Nick   I'm a bond man.

Tom   Who with?

Nick   Channing and Locke.

Tom   Never heard of them.

Nick   You will, if you stay in the East.

Tom   Oh, I'll stay in the East, don't you worry. I'd be a goddamned fool not to.

Jordan   Absolutely! (*She yawns extravagantly.*) I've been lying here as long as I can remember.

Daisy   Get the girl a drink, won't you, Tom?

Jordan   No thanks. I'm absolutely in training.

Tom (*downing his own drink*)   Ha! How you ever get anything done is beyond me.

Jordan   Self-discipline. (*To* **Nick**.) You live in West Egg. I know somebody there.

Nick   I don't know a single soul.

Jordan   You must know Gatsby.

Daisy (*starting*)   Gatsby? What Gatsby?

Servant   Dinner is served, sir, madame.

Nick   The evening processed. I enjoyed looking at Miss Baker, wondering what it was that she '*got done*'.

I had seen her somewhere before. Tom spoke often and in his gruff, contemptuous tenor, familiar to me from college where he'd wielded it as a weapon, even toward people who liked him – and there were plenty who hated his guts. As for Daisy – her face was sad and lovely, and in her voice a kind of promise, of bright things, excitement. Then of a sudden, after dinner was over –

Daisy (*showing her hand*)   Look – I hurt it. Or Tom did, rather.

Jordan   It's black and blue!

Daisy   I know you didn't mean to. It's what I get for marrying a brute of a man, a great big hulking physical specimen –

Tom   I hate that word hulking, even in kidding.

Daisy   Hulking!

Nick   The word hung in the air.

Daisy and Miss Baker talked about the social season in New York, with a bantering inconsequence as cool as their white dresses . . .

Tom (*pulling* **Nick** *aside*)   Listen, have you read 'The Rise of the Colored Empires', by this man Goddard?

Nick   Why, no.

Tom   Well, it's a fine book, everybody ought to read it. The idea is, if we don't look out the white race will be utterly submerged.

The phone rings, off.

It's scientifically proven. It's up to us, the dominant race, to watch out. We're Nordics, you know – I am, you are, they are – and we've produced all the things that go to make civilisation – science, art, and all that. Do you see?

A **Servant** *has entered.*

Servant   Excuse me, sir. A telephone call for you.

Tom *leaves.*

Daisy   Oh Nick, it's adorable to see you here.

Nick   I'm very glad to be here.

Daisy   You remind me of a – of a rose. An absolute rose. Doesn't he, darling?

Daisy *gets up quickly and leaves.*

Nick   Well, no one ever compared me to a rose before.

Jordan (*straining to hear the voices, off*)   Sshh.

Nick   This Mr Gatsby you spoke of is my neighbour –

Jordan (*gestures 'wait'*)   I want to hear what happens!

Nick   Is something happening?

Jordan   Tom's got some woman in New York.

They listen.

She might have the decency not to telephone him at dinner time. Don't you think so?

The voices off rise in temperature. Then stop. **Daisy** *comes back in.*

Daisy   I looked outside, it's very romantic – there's a bird on the lawn, singing away. I think it must be a nightingale come over on the White Star Line. We don't know each other very well, Nick, even if we are cousins. You didn't come to my wedding.

Nick   I wasn't back from the war.

Daisy   Well, I've had a very bad time, and I'm pretty cynical about everything. When my girl was born – do you want to know what I said?

Nick   Very much.

Daisy   Tom was God knows where. I woke up out of the ether feeling utterly abandoned. And when the nurse told me it was a girl, I wept. 'I'm so glad', I said. 'And I hope she'll be a fool – that's the best thing a girl can be in this world, a beautiful little fool.'

Jordan   I'll drink to that.

Daisy   Everything's terrible anyhow, don't you think so? Everybody's saying it – the most advanced people.

Tom *has come back.*

Daisy   And I *know* it's true. I've been everywhere and seen everything and done everything. (*She laughs.*) Sophisticated – God, I'm sophisticated!

Tom (*to* **Nick**)   Come to lunch with me in the city tomorrow. We'll take the train.

Nick   I'd like that.

Jordan   Time for this good girl to go to bed.

Daisy   Jordan's playing in the big golf tournament over at Westchester tomorrow –

Nick   Oh, you're *Jor*dan Baker –

Jordan   For my sins. Wake me at eight, won't you?

Daisy   I'll try!

Nick   Good luck.

Jordan   Nice to meet you, Mr Carraway. See you around.

Daisy   Of course you will. I'll arrange your marriage.

Jordan (*kissing* **Daisy**)   Good night. Good night.

Tom   Good night.

Jordan *goes*.

Tom   She's a nice girl, but the way her people let her run around the country this way –

Daisy   Her 'people' is one aunt about a thousand years old. Besides, Nick's going to look after her, aren't you, Nick?

Nick   Is she from New York?

Daisy   Louisville. We passed our lily-white girlhood together. So I forgot to ask you something important. Were you engaged to a girl out West?

Nick   Me?

Tom   That's what we heard.

Nick   It's a libel.

Daisy   Oh?

Nick   I'm much too poor to be engaged.

Daisy   But we heard it from at least three people, so it must be true.

Nick   Their interest rather touched me and made them seem less remotely rich – nevertheless as I thanked them for dinner and made my way to my car I had a confusion of feelings – among them abhorrence. In my mind's eye I saw Daisy rush out of the house, child in arms, never to look back. But there were apparently no such thoughts in her head. As for Tom, the fact that he had a woman in New York was frankly less surprising than that he had been depressed by a book.

I reached my kingdom on the other side of the bay and sat a while in the yard. The air was full of moonlight, with wings beating in the trees. A cat was stalking the lawn. As I watched it, I saw I was not alone – not fifty feet away Mr Gatsby was standing with his hands in his pockets, surveying his portion of our local heavens. And I was about to call to him, when he stretched out his arms toward the dark water. I glanced seaward – I could make out a single green light, minute and far away – it might have been the end of a dock. When I looked back, Gatsby had vanished.

Scene Two

Nick *and* **Tom** *are on the train.* **Tom** *is drunk, and he takes nips from a flask.*

Tom What do you think of the view? To think, people live out in these parts.

Nick Must be what it's like to live on the moon.

Tom All the garbage of New York, burned to ash and piled mountain high.

Nick It's awfully grim.

Tom We're getting off.

Nick What?

Tom Come on! I want you to meet my girl.

Nick He literally forced me from the train and marched me two hundred yards down a dirt road, under the baleful

gaze of a pair of gigantic eyes painted on a billboard –
DR T. J. ECKLEBURG, it said, OCULIST. Evidently the
good doctor set them there to fatten his practice in the
borough of Queens, and –

Tom   Hello Wilson, old man – how's business?

Wilson   I can't complain. When are you going to sell me
that car?

Tom   My man's working on it still.

Wilson   Works pretty slow, don't he?

Tom   If you feel that way, maybe I'd better go
somewhere else.

Wilson   I didn't mean that – I just meant –

Myrtle (*comes in*)   Get some chairs, why don't you, so
somebody can sit down.

Wilson   Oh, sure –

And he goes.

Tom (*to* **Myrtle**)   I want to see you. Get on the next train.

Myrtle   All right.

Tom (*takes a note from his wallet, stuffs it in her sleeve or
pocket*)   Here's for a cab.

Myrtle   I love you.

Nick   So Tom Buchanan and his girl and I went up to New
York – Mrs Wilson sat discreetly in another car, and made
her own way to the apartment he kept for her at West 158th
Street. I worked up the courage to ask:

Doesn't her husband object?

Tom   What, Wilson? He thinks she goes to see her sister.
He's so dumb he doesn't know he's alive.

The party at West 158th Street. Music – Three O'Clock in the Morning.

Everybody drinks through the whole scene.

Nick (*to us*) This is Mr Chester McKee, a professional musician who lives downstairs –

Chester How do you do?

Nick And Myrtle's sister Catherine.

Catherine *gives a drunken curtsey.*

Nick It was my surmise that these two were not attached. Tom and Myrtle meanwhile disappeared into a bedroom . . . I have been drunk just twice in my life, and the second time was that afternoon.

They drink, and dance.

The world beyond the apartment receded, and time became a matter of your point of view.

Nick (*to* **Catherine**) Do you live here too?

Catherine *bursts out laughing.*

Catherine Do I live here? No, I share a room with a girlfriend in the Vermont, round the corner. What about you?

Nick I live at West Egg.

Catherine Really? I was just down there at a party. At a man named Gatsby's. You been to Gatsby's?

Nick No, but I live next door to him.

Catherine You do? He's a nephew of the German Kaiser.

Nick Is that so?

Catherine That's where all his money comes from. He scares me. I'd hate to have him get anything on me.

Chester When do you think they'll be done, in there?

Catherine   Why don't you give us *The Love Nest*, Chester? That'll flush 'em out.

Chester   An excellent suggestion.

Chester *plays and sings* The Love Nest.

Catherine   Neither of them can stand the person they're married to.

Nick   Can't they?

Catherine   Can't *stand* them. What I say is, why go on living with them if they can't stand them?

Myrtle *enters, now in a chiffon dress.*

Myrtle   Did the elevator boy come with my cigarettes? God damn these people.

Myrtle *goes.*

Catherine   It's really his wife that's keeping them apart.

Nick   Tom's wife?

Catherine   She's a Catholic, they don't believe in divorce.

Nick *aside.*

Nick   Daisy wasn't a Catholic, and I was a little shocked at the lie.

Catherine   When they do get married they're going West till it all blows over.

They listen to **Chester** *singing a verse of the song.* **Myrtle** *comes in.*

Catherine   Why did you marry George?

Myrtle   I married him because –

Catherine   Nobody forced you to.

Myrtle   I thought he was a gentleman.

Catherine   You were crazy about him.

Myrtle   He wasn't fit to lick my shoe. I was no more crazy about him than I was about that man there.

She points at **Nick**.

Nick   Not guilty.

Myrtle   I knew right away I made a mistake. He borrowed somebody's best suit, a man came for it one day when he was out. 'Oh, is that your suit?' I said. And I gave it to him and cried to beat the band all afternoon. Tom? Tom, let us have some more of that whiskey, would you –

Nick   I wanted to get out, walk in the Park through the soft twilight, but each time I tried I became entangled in some wild, strident argument. It was ten o'clock. Some celebrated sandwiches arrived with a fresh batch of liquor and we fell on them like hobos. It was eleven o'clock. I got into an absurd state. Around twelve thirty I was explaining Treasury bonds to Mr McKee (as I understood them) when –

Tom   Don't you say her name!

Myrtle   Why not? It's a free country! Daisy!

Tom   Don't you say her name, goddamn you!

Myrtle   Daisy! Daisy!

Tom   Shut up!

Myrtle   Daisy! I'll say her name whenever I want to! Daisy! Dai –

Tom *hits* **Myrtle** *in the face, knocking her to the floor. Screams and consternation.*

Tom *disappears.* **Chester** *and* **Nick** *and* **Catherine** *help* **Myrtle**. *There is blood.*

An orchestral version of Three O'Clock in the Morning *starts up.*

Catherine *leads* **Myrtle** *off.* **Chester** *pours two glasses.*

Chester   Your good health, Nick.

Nick And to yours.

They toast one another and down their drinks. Then they dance, cheek to cheek.

Lights fade, with the music.

Scene Three

Gatsby's mansion, one week later.

Music and dancing.

Gatsby (*voiceover*)   Dear Mr Carraway,

Please forgive me, neighbour. I have seen you several times and meant to call on you to introduce myself, but a peculiar combination of circumstances has prevented it. I am giving a little party this evening, Saturday. If you are able to attend the honor will be entirely mine. Jay Gatsby.

Jordan *dances with a partygoer called* **Sarah**.

Sarah Excuse me – aren't you Jordan Baker?

Jordan Possibly!

Sarah I'm sorry you didn't win the other day!

Jordan So am I!

Sarah I was rooting for you!

Jordan I love your dress!

Sarah Isn't it just peachy keen? I tore mine the last time I was here – Mr Gatsby asked for my address and the very next day this one came, brand new in the box! Two hundred and sixty five dollars – Oh, goodness!

Jordan What is it?

Sarah Mary! – she's doing handstands in the fountain!

She pulls **Jordan** *to her, and they kiss.*

Sarah   You're lovely, by the way –

Sarah *runs away.* **Nick** *enters, in evening dress*

Jordan   I thought I might run into you.

Nick   Who was that?

Jordan   I haven't the first idea.

Nick   It's like an amusement park out here.

Jordan   Hardly. Who arrives at an amusement park in a Rolls Royce laid on by the management?

Nick   And what amusement park has a seventy piece orchestra? Or a battalion of caterers?

Jordan *swipes two cocktails from a passing tray.*

Jordan   Not to mention a first-class bar?

Nick   We won't mention it.

They clink glasses.

Jordan   It's good to see you, Nick.

Nick   Likewise.

Jordan   What's the matter?

Nick   The matter?

Jordan   You're nervous.

Nick   I am a little.

Jordan   I know why.

Nick   You do?

Jordan   You haven't met the host yet. Come on.

They go.

Chorus   The orchestra plays yellow cocktail music
And the opera of voices pitches a key higher
There goes Benny McClenahan
He always comes with three girls

Never the same three
Their first names Judy or June or Jacqueline
Connie, Clara, Consuela
And their last, the stern syllables of the great American
capitalists
Whose cousins, if pressed, they will confess themselves to be.
The air is alive
With gossip and chatter
And casual innuendo
And introductions forgotten on the spot
As dancers dance
Lovers withdraw to upper rooms
Happy, vacuous laughter rises toward the summer sky
And the moon turns her face away, discreetly.

Nick *and* **Jordan** *enter the library, where they find* **Owl-Eyes**
sitting on the floor with a book. **Owl-Eyes** *can be a man or a*
woman but whoever they are they are very drunk.

Owl-Eyes   What do you think?

Jordan   About what?

Owl-Eyes   The books – they're real. Bona-fide printed
matter. How about that?

Jordan   Well, it *is* a library.

Owl-Eyes   I thought they'd be fake! This fella's a one for
theatrical detail, I'll give him that. He's a bootlegger,
probably. Good for him. Who brought you? Or did you just
come? I was brought. I've been drunk for about a week now,
and I thought it might sober me up to sit in a library.

Nick (*giving* **Owl-Eyes** *a hand up*)   And has it?

Owl-Eyes (*unsteadily*)   Certainly. Now I'm so hungry I could
eat your buttonhole.

Jordan   Come on, let's go downstairs.

Owl-Eyes   What's downstairs?

Jordan   Second supper.

Owl-Eyes   Ah, I love second supper!

Nick   I wasn't hungry for lobster or steak or any of the other myriad offerings at second supper so I rejoined the fray outside. To my astonishment, there were still more parties arriving in cars, and fresh gatherings were breaking out all over the gardens. In one of the marquees, a notorious author and his even more notorious wife were singing an obscene and satirical duet of their own composition to an audience of around a hundred, who roared their approval. Then fireworks went off on the stroke of midnight and somebody shouted –

Somebody   It's my birthday!

Nick   – setting off another caravansary of festivities. Champagne was in bowls, not glasses – I had taken two of them and everything was turning golden and elemental and significant.

Gatsby   Your face is familiar. Weren't you in the Third Division during the war?

Nick   Yes, I was – ninth machine-gun battalion.

Gatsby   I knew I'd seen you somewhere before.

Nick   Were you in France, in '18?

Gatsby   Surely – were you at Argonne Forest?

Nick   I was back home before that.

Gatsby   Good for you.

Nick   Well, well. How d'you do?

Gatsby   Say – I just bought a hydroplane.

Nick   Really?

Gatsby   Want to go up with me tomorrow, old sport? Just near the shore along the Sound.

Jordan *enters*.

Nick   What time?

Gatsby   Any time that suits you best.

Jordan   Better now, Mr Carraway?

Nick   Much. (*To* **Gatsby**.) Though I still haven't seen the host. I live across the road, you see, and this man Gatsby sent over his chauffeur with an invitation.

Gatsby   I'm Gatsby.

Nick   I beg your pardon –

Gatsby   I thought you knew, old sport. I'm afraid I'm not a very good host.

A **Butler** *comes to* **Gatsby**'s *elbow, clears his throat and says, softly.*

Butler   Chicago is calling you on the wire, sir.

Gatsby   If you want anything, just ask for it. Excuse me.

Nick   Who is he? Do you know?

Jordan   He's just a man named Gatsby.

Nick   Where is he from, I mean? And what does he do?

Jordan   Now *you're* hooked on the subject just like everyone else.

Nick   Evidently.

Jordan   He told me once he was an Oxford man.

Nick   Really?

Jordan   I don't believe it, either.

Nick   I did for a moment.

Jordan   Anyhow, he gives large parties –

Nick   This much is indisputable.

Jordan   And I like large parties. They're so intimate.

Nick   Young men don't just drift out of nowhere and buy a palace –

Treves (*comes up to* **Jordan**)   Forgive me. It's Jordan Baker, isn't it?

Jordan   Why, yes.

Treves (*offering his hand*)   Sheldon Treves, delighted. Now look, I hate to be one of those people who bothers you but may I have an autograph for my niece?

Jordan   Certainly.

Treves   She's learning the game and she thinks you're the bees knees and so do I. And no matter what that caddy said he saw or thought he might have seen – well we just know you always play fair. (*He can't find paper in his pockets.*) Would you have anything to write on?

Nick *and* **Jordan** *apologise, but they don't.*

Treves   Just sign my cuff, here, that'll be all right.

Jordan   Do you have a pen?

Treves   A pen. Damn it. Do you? (**Nick** *and* **Jordan** *shrug,* **Treves** *says to* **Jordan**, *aside.*) I want to give you my number in New York.

Anybody got a pen? (**Treves** *wanders off.*) A pen! A pen!

Nick   What it is to be famous!

Jordan   Don't I know.

Butler *returns.*

Butler   Miss Baker? I beg your pardon, but Mr Gatsby would like to speak with you alone.

Jordan   With me?

Butler   Yes, madame.

Jordan *shares a raised-eyebrow moment with* **Nick**, *then goes with the* **Butler**.

Nick   The stranger's remark about the caddy – *now* I
remembered the story about Jordan Baker that had eluded
me ever since that night at Daisy's. At a big tournament in
the spring there was a row that reached the newspapers – a
suggestion she had moved her ball from a bad lie in the
semi-final round. It blew up into a scandal – then it blew
over. A caddy retracted his statement and Jordan was
cleared. Out of the rough, you might say.

A singer (accompanied) gives a raucous rendition of The Sheik of
Araby. **Nick** *applauds with the rest.*

Nick   Three o'clock in the morning and the waltz by that
name was starting up in the ballroom. Time to collect my hat
and walk back to my domain –

Jordan *and* **Gatsby** *come in together.*

Gatsby   Hello, old sport.

Jordan   Are you leaving soon?

Nick   Shortly.

Jordan   I'll drive you.

Nick   Drive me? But –

Jordan   I insist.

Nick   Mr Gatsby – thank you for a wonderful evening, really.

Gatsby   I'm very glad you could make it.

Nick   I do apologise for not knowing you, earlier.

Gatsby   Don't mention it. And don't forget we're going up
in the hydroplane this morning, old sport, nine o'clock.
Good night, good night.

Gatsby *goes.*

Jordan   I've just heard the most amazing thing. How long
were we in there?

Nick (*taking his hat*)   About an hour?

Jordan   Come on.

They go.

Engine rev, car horn toot. They are sitting in **Jordan**'s *car, and she's driving.*

Jordan   It was simply . . . amazing.

Nick   I believe you. You don't have to go so fast, you know.

Jordan   I enjoy it.

Nick   Hey – we're here! – stop!

Jordan   But I only just started!

Nick   Jordan! That was my house!

Jordan   That's too short a ride. We have to go round the bay.

Nick   And back again.

Jordan   And back again. Don't worry.

Nick   I've got to get some sleep before I fly in his plane, in, what, five hours?

Jordan   You ever flown before?

Nick   No.

Jordan   You're going to love it.

Nick   So it was amazing, whatever it was.

Jordan   It was.

Nick   But you can't say anything more about it.

Jordan   He made me swear. Sorry.

Nick   Look out for that car, ahead.

Jordan!

Nick *lunges for the wheel and turns it, to avoid a collision, screech of brakes and screaming of horns.*

My god, but you're a rotten driver.

Jordan   Who says I am?

Nick   You ought to be more careful, or you oughtn't drive at all.

Jordan   I am careful.

Nick   Ha!

Jordan   Well, other people are.

Nick   What's that got to do with it?

Jordan   They keep out of my way. It takes two to make an accident.

Nick   Suppose you met somebody just as careless as yourself?

Jordan   I hope I never will. I hate careless people. That's why I like you.

They kiss, passionately. Lights fade. In the scene change, the sound of engines, gears, rasping horns and police sirens, to a cacophonous crescendo.

Scene Four

Gatsby *is driving* **Nick**.

Nick   Over the next few weeks I talked with Gatsby perhaps six times, at his parties. And I found, to my disappointment, that he had little to say. Still, I liked him very much. His epic generosity, his decorous if slightly over-deliberate manners, and his golden smile – all of these were pleasing parts and the sum was – Gatsby. Then one morning late in July he invited me to take lunch with him in the city.

Gatsby   What do you think of my car, old sport? Pretty, isn't it?

Nick   God, yes. It's beautiful.

Pause.

Nick   Further pleasantries for several miles, back and forth, as the engine sang. We fell quiet, and I was almost sleepy, when –

Gatsby   Look here, old sport. What's your opinion of me, anyhow?

Nick   My *opinion* of you? Why, that's a question to ask a fellow –

Gatsby   I'm going to tell you something about my life. I don't want you to get the wrong idea of me from all these stories you hear.

Nick   All right –

Gatsby   I'll tell you God's truth. I am the son of some wealthy people in the Middle West – all dead now. I was brought up in America but educated at – at Oxford, because all my ancestors have been educated there for many years. It's a family tradition.

Nick   What part of the Middle West?

Gatsby   San Francisco.

Nick   I see.

Gatsby   My family all died and I came into a good deal of money. After that I lived like a young rajah in all the capitals of Europe – Paris, Venice, London – collecting jewels, chiefly rubies, hunting big game, painting a little, and trying to forget something very sad that happened to me long ago.

Nick   I almost burst out laughing. From the moment he fumbled over the Oxford thing his story was ever more ridiculous. San Francisco in the Mid West? Big game in Europe? I pictured him in a bejewelled turban, stalking tigers in Kensington Gardens.

Gatsby   Then came the war, old sport. It was a great relief, and I tried very hard to die, but I seemed to bear an enchanted life. In the Argonne I led two machine-gun detachments so far forward that the infantry couldn't support us. A hundred and thirty men under me with sixteen Lewis guns. Two days and two nights later the infantry finally reached us and among the German dead they found the insignia of three divisions. Well, I was promoted after that, and every Allied government gave me a decoration – (**Gatsby** *pulls a medal and ribbon from his pocket, hands it to* **Nick**.) – even little Montenegro, down on the Adriatic Sea!

Nick (*reads*)   'Major Jay Gatsby. For Valour Extraordinary'.

Gatsby (*taking out a photograph*)   Here's another thing I always carry. A souvenir of Oxford days.

Nick   That's you, with the cricket bat.

Gatsby   The man on my left is now the Earl of Doncaster.

Nick   Then it was all true? I saw him in his palace on the Grand Canal, staring into a casket of rubies to ease the gnawings of his broken heart . . .

Gatsby   I'm going to make a big request of you today, so I thought you ought to know something about me. I don't want you to think I'm just some nobody. You see, I usually find myself among strangers because I drift here and there trying to forget the sad thing that happened to me. You'll hear about it this afternoon.

Nick   At lunch?

Gatsby   I happened to find out that you're taking Miss Baker to tea.

Nick   You're in love with Jordan?

Gatsby   No, old sport, I'm not. But she has kindly consented to speak to you about this matter.

Nick   And with that, he was done. I hadn't the faintest idea what this 'matter' could be but I was rather annoyed than intrigued – I hadn't asked Jordan to tea to talk about Mr Jay Gatsby. We sped on through the valley of ashes, past Wilson's garage and the giant eyes of Dr Eckleburg keeping their solemn vigil. Then at last – the great view of the city from the Queensboro Bridge, promising all the mystery and beauty in the world. Anything can happen now, I thought to myself. Anything at all.

Scene Five

A restaurant in Manhattan, 42nd Street. **Gatsby** *and* **Meyer Wolfshiem** *in conference.* **Nick** *joins them.*

Gatsby   Mr Carraway, glad you could join us. This is my friend Mr Wolfshiem.

Wolfshiem (*shaking* **Nick**'s *hand*)   So I took one look at him, and what do you think I did? I handed the money to Katspaugh and I said All right, Katspaugh, don't pay him a penny till he shuts his mouth. He shut it then and there.

Nick   I'm sure he did.

Wolfshiem   This is a nice restaurant, but I like across the street better!

Gatsby   It's too hot over there.

Wolfshiem   You're right. But full of memories.

Nick   What place is that?

Wolfshiem   The old Metropole. Filled with faces dead and gone. I can't forget so long as I live the night they shot Rosy Rosenthal there. There's six of us at the dinner table, and Rosy has ate and drunk a lot all evening. Now the waiter comes with a funny look in his eye and says to him, 'Mr Rosenthal, somebody wants to speak with you outside.' 'Let the bastards come in here if they want you, Rosy,' I say. But he says, 'Don't let them take away my coffee,' and goes out on the sidewalk. They shoot him three times in his full belly and drive away.

Nick   I remember the story.

Wolfshiem   Five of them were electrocuted. I understand you're looking for a business gonnegtion.

Gatsby   No, Meyer – this isn't the man.

Wolfshiem   No?

Gatsby   This is just a friend.

Wolfshiem   I beg your pardon. I had a wrong man.

Wolfshiem *gets up and leaves.*

Gatsby   I'm afraid I made you a little angry in the car this morning, old sport.

Nick   I don't like mysteries, that's all. Why has it all got to come through Miss Baker?

Gatsby   It's nothing underhand – she's a great sportswoman, you know – she'd never do anything that wasn't all right –

Wolfshiem *comes back, scoffing a bowl of olives or some other bar snack.* **Gatsby** *looks at his watch and hurries out.*

Wolfshiem   Fine fellow, isn't he? A perfect gentleman.

Nick   He is.

Wolfshiem   He went to Oggsford College, in England.

Nick   Have you known him long?

Wolfshiem   Since just after the war. I said to myself, 'Here's a man you could take home and introduce to your mother and sisters'. I see you're looking at my cuff buttons. Finest specimens of human molars.

Nick   That's a very interesting idea.

Wolfshiem   Yeah, Gatsby's very careful about women. He would never so much as look at a friend's wife. (**Gatsby** *comes back*.) Now. I have enjoyed your company, and I'm going to run off from you two young men so you can order your lunch and discuss your sports and your young ladies and all your other business.

Gatsby   Don't hurry, Meyer.

Wolfshiem   You're very polite, but I won't impose on you any longer.

Wolfshiem *shakes their hands and leaves.*

Gatsby   Meyer's quite a character around Broadway.

Nick   Who is he, anyhow, an actor?

Gatsby   No.

Nick   A dentist?

Gatsby   Meyer Wolfshiem? No, he's a gambler. He's the man who fixed the World's Series, in '19.

Nick *is stunned.*

Nick   He fixed the World's Series? – That was *him*? How'd he do it?

Gatsby   He just saw the opportunity.

Nick   Why isn't he in jail?

Gatsby   They can't get him, old sport. He's a smart man.

Nick *sees* **Tom** *across the room, and stands.*

Nick   My oh my, I do believe –

Tom *comes bounding towards them.*

Tom   What do you say about that!

Nick   It's a small world.

Tom   Where've you been?

Nick   This is Mr Gatsby, Mr Buchanan.

Tom *and* **Gatsby** *shake hands, say how d'you do.*

Tom (*to* **Nick**)   Daisy's rather furious with you for not calling up.

Nick   I have meant to. The thing is, I've had rather a lot of work –

Tom   Wall Street, huh. What else have you been doing? Improving your swing with Jordan, I hear? Well, good for you. How d'you happen to come up this far to eat?

Nick   Mr Gatsby invited me to lunch with a friend of his, it's one of his favourite places. Isn't that so –?

They turn to **Gatsby** *– but he's left.*

Scene Six

The tea room at the Plaza Hotel. **Jordan** *sits upright,* **Nick** *stands and listens.*

Jordan   Are you standing uncomfortably? Then I'll begin. One October day – this was in '17 – I noticed Daisy Fay's little roadster beside the curb – and there she was in a white dress, sitting with a lieutenant I'd never seen before. Daisy was by far the most popular girl in Louisville, impossibly glamorous, and here was this officer looking at her in a way that every girl wants to be looked at some time. She called me over and introduced us. Lieutenant Jay Gatsby.

I didn't lay eyes on him again for over four years – even then I didn't realize it was the same man.

Spin forward a year, I was playing in tournaments so didn't see so much of Daisy but I heard the rumours, how her mother found her packing a bag one winter night to go to New York and say goodbye to a soldier who was going overseas. Her family absolutely forbade her and they fell out over it. But it all blew over and she had a debut in '18, after the Armistice, and in June of '19 she married one Thomas Buchanan of Chicago, with more pomp and circumstance than Louisville ever knew before. He brought a hundred people down, and the day before the wedding he gave Daisy a string of pearls valued at – guess.

Nick   I couldn't. Twenty thousand?

Jordan   Three hundred and fifty thousand dollars. (**Nick** *whistles*.) But listen to this. I was a bridesmaid, and a half hour before the bridal dinner I came into her room and she was lying on her bed, lovely as the June night – and drunk.

Nick   Daisy was?

Jordan   A bottle of Sauterne in one hand and a letter in the other and she says, "Gratulate me, Jordan. Never had a drink before but oh, how I do enjoy it!' Then she gropes around in a waste-basket she has on the bed and pulls out the string of pearls: 'Take 'em back downstairs and tell 'em all Daisy's change' her mine!' Then she cried and she cried. Her mother's maid and I, we got her into a cold bath. But she wouldn't stop crying and she wouldn't let go of that letter. She squeezed it into a wet ball till it came to pieces like snow. We gave her spirits of ammonia and set about dressing her and a half hour later she walked out into that party with those pearls around her neck.

Nick   And she married Tom.

Jordan   Five o'clock the next day, without so much as a shiver.

Nick   They honeymooned in the South Seas, as I recall.

Jordan   I saw them when they came back – this was in Santa Barbara – and I honestly thought I'd never seen a girl so mad about her husband. If he left the room for a minute she'd say, 'Where's Tom gone?' It was touching to see them together – it made you laugh in a hushed, fascinated sort of way. Then came the accident.

Nick   The accident?

Jordan   Tom crashed his car into a wagon on the Ventura road, ripped a front wheel off. It got into the papers, because the girl was injured –

Nick   What girl?

Jordan   A chambermaid at the Santa Barbara Hotel.

Nick   I see.

Jordan   The next April, Daisy had her little girl, and they went to France for a year. I saw them over there, in Cannes. Then last year, they came back to Chicago. They moved with a fast crowd, all of them young and rich and wild, but Daisy came out with an absolutely perfect reputation. Perhaps because she doesn't drink – it's a great advantage not to drink among hard-drinking people. All of which brings us to about six weeks ago, when she heard the name Gatsby for the first time in years.

Nick   When you asked me if I knew him.

Jordan   Yes. And that night she came and woke me and she said, 'This Gatsby, describe him'. It was so strange. I thought I was dreaming. Then I realized. He was the officer in her car.

Nick   It was a strange coincidence.

Jordan   Nick? It wasn't at all. Don't you see?

Gatsby bought that house so Daisy would be just across the bay.

Music. During the following the scene is set for **Daisy** *and* **Gatsby's** *meeting at* **Nick's** *house. Tea things, flowers.*

Nick (*aside*)   Gatsby came alive to me – delivered from the womb of his purposeless splendour.

Jordan   He wants you to invite Daisy to your house some afternoon and then let him come over.

Nick   Is that all?

Jordan   He's afraid, he's waited so long. He thought you might be offended.

Nick   Why didn't he ask *you* to arrange a meeting?

Jordan   He wants her to see his house – and there's a fine view of it from your place.

Nick   Oh!

Jordan   I think he half expected her to wander into one of his parties, some night. But she never did. He began asking people casually if they knew her, and I was the first one he found.

Nick   Do you think she'll want to see him?

Jordan   She's not to know about it. You're just supposed to invite her for tea.

Nick   A phrase began to beat in my brain: There are only the pursued, the pursuing, the busy, and the tired.

Scene Seven

Distant rolls of thunder. **Gatsby** *paces the room, checking his watch.*

Nick   It was ten before four on the day agreed upon, and pouring rain. I'd invited Daisy for tea at four.

Gatsby   Is everything all right?

Nick   I think so.

Gatsby   The hot water.

Nick   What about it?

Gatsby   There's enough?

Nick   To float a battleship. Do you like lemon cake?

Gatsby (*testily*)   Do I what?

Nick   The lemon cake, I was asking you if –

Gatsby   Of course! It's fine!

An awkward pause.

Listen here, old sport, you don't make much money, do you?

Nick   Not very much.

Gatsby   Pardon my – you see, I carry on a little business on the side – You're selling bonds, aren't you?

Nick   Trying to.

Gatsby   Well, this would interest you and you might pick up a nice bit of money. It happens to be a rather confidential sort of thing.

Nick (*aside*)   For services rendered. For a liaison with my cousin who happened to be married.

Gatsby   You wouldn't have to do any business with Wolfshiem.

Nick   I'm much obliged but – I've got my hands full.

Gatsby   All right, old sport.

Gatsby *continues his pacing* . . .

Nick   He was in a kind of agony. At two minutes to four –

Gatsby   I'm going home.

Nick   Why?

Gatsby   Nobody's coming to tea. It's too late!

Nick   Don't be silly, it's not even four –

Gatsby   I can't wait all day.

Gatsby *makes as if to go. Sound of an engine, pulling up outside.* **Gatsby** *retreats out of sight.*

Nick *opens the door to* **Daisy**.

Daisy   Nick!

They kiss hello.

Nick   Lovely weather we're having.

Daisy   I adore it. Is this absolutely where you live, my dearest one?

Nick   I do apologise.

Daisy   Nonsense – it's charming! But why did I have to come alone? (*Mock-serious.*) Are you in love with me, darling?

Nick   Ah, now, you see – this is the secret of Castle Rackrent –

Gatsby *walks solemnly and steadily into the room.*

A pause.

Daisy   Hello, Jay.

Gatsby   Hello.

Daisy   This is a surprise.

Gatsby   I hope you're not upset by it.

Daisy   Of course not.

I am awfully glad to see you again.

Music.

Lights fade.

INTERVAL

Scene Eight

The scene as before. **Gatsby** *is fiddling with his pocket watch.*

Gatsby   We've met before.

Daisy   Some years ago, as a matter of fact.

Gatsby   Five years next November.

Nick (*aside*)   Nothing much more of any significance was said for what seemed to me like a full hour, though it could only have been five minutes.

Gatsby *drops his watch.*

Daisy   Oh!

Gatsby   Please forgive me.

Daisy   Is it all right?

Gatsby   It's not important.

Nick *edges toward the door.*

Nick   Excuse me won't you, I must just –

Gatsby   Where are you going?

Nick   I'll be back.

Gatsby   I've got to speak to you about something before you go.

Gatsby *follows* **Nick**.

Nick   What is it?

Gatsby   This is a terrible mistake.

Nick   You're just embarrassed, that's all. She's embarrassed too.

Gatsby   She is?

Nick   And you're acting like a little boy about it. A rude one, at that. Go back in there and talk to her.

Gatsby *goes back in.*

Nick   I left by the back door and bolted through the rain, for the umbrella of a huge knotted tree. There was nothing to look at except that enormous house of his, so I stared at it, like Kant at his church steeple, for a half hour. He told me

later it took him just three years to earn the money that
bought it – from what enterprising business he declined to
say. The sun came out eventually, and a grocer delivered
to the house, and a maid began opening the upper windows,
one by one, leaning out to drink the brightening air.
Then she spat into the garden, meditatively. It was time I
went back.

I made every possible noise in the kitchen, before pushing
open the door. They were looking at each other as if a
question was in the air –

Gatsby   Oh hello, old sport.

Nick   It's stopped raining.

Gatsby   Has it? (*To* **Daisy**.) What do you think of that?

Daisy   I'm glad, Jay.

Nick   Daisy's face was smeared with tears, and there was a
change in Gatsby that was simply confounding –

Gatsby   I want you and Daisy to come over to my house, I'd
like to show her around.

Nick   You're sure you want me to come?

Gatsby   Absolutely, old sport.

Nick   Instead of taking the short cut along the Sound
we went down to the road and entered Gatsby's estate by
the great gate. The mansion shimmered in the haze after
the rain.

Daisy   You mean to say – that huge place?

Gatsby   Do you like it?

Daisy   I love it.

Nick   As we wandered through the music-rooms and the
salons, I felt as if there were guests concealed behind every
couch and every table, under orders to be silent while we
passed. I watched Gatsby, watching Daisy – and revaluing

everything in every room on every floor, by the response it
drew from her.

Gatsby (*laughing*)   It's the funniest thing, old sport. I can't –
when I try to –

Nick   He had been full of the idea so long, dreamed it right
through to the end, at an inconceivable pitch of intensity.
And now – now he was running down like an overwound
clock.

Daisy *is admiring* **Gatsby**'*s clothes, laid out in piles.*

Daisy   They're such beautiful shirts!

Gatsby   I have a man in England who buys me clothes.

Daisy   Do you really?

Gatsby   He sends over a selection of things at the beginning
of each season, spring and fall.

Daisy *starts to cry.*

Daisy   They make me sad because – because – I've never
seen such beautiful shirts before –

Music – Who's Sorry Now?

Nick   In another room, he showed her a volume of
clippings he'd collected over the past several years –

Gatsby   They're all about you.

The phone rings, **Gatsby** *goes and answers it.*

Yes . . . Well, I can't talk now . . . I said I can't talk, old sport
. . . I said a *small* town . . . He must know what a small town is
. . . Well, he's no use to us if Detroit is his idea of a small
town . . .

Nick   Soon after, they stood side by side at a window
watching the rain, falling again from a bar of darkness –

Daisy   Look at that. I'd like to get one of those pink clouds
and put you in it and push you around.

Gatsby   If it wasn't for the mist we could see your home across the bay. You always have a green light that burns all night at the end of your dock.

Nick   I wanted to take my leave but they wouldn't hear of it – I think my being there made them feel more satisfactorily alone.

Daisy   Does he really live here all by himself, Nick?

Gatsby   Oh, I keep it always full of interesting people, night and day – isn't it so?

Nick   He does.

Daisy   What kind of people?

Gatsby   People who do interesting things. Celebrated people.

Scene Nine

Music. Saturday night. One of Gatsby's parties – and actually, this is to be the last, ever. **Daisy** *and* **Nick** *are practising a dance move.* **Tom** *surveys the scene.* **Gatsby** *hands him a cigar.*

Daisy   These things excite me *so*. If you want to kiss me any time during the evening, Nick, just let me know –

Gatsby   Look around.

Daisy   I am looking around. I'm already having a marvellous –

Gatsby   You must see the faces of many people you've heard about.

Tom   We don't go around very much. I don't believe I know a soul here.

Gatsby   Perhaps you know that lady, under the tree.

Daisy   Oh! Is it really her?

Gatsby   The man beside her is her director.

Nick   We stared at the famous movie actress – a gorgeous, scarcely human orchid of a woman, sat in state on a high-backed chair. A shiver passed through us – surely she couldn't be flesh and blood?

Gatsby steered them through the crowd, introducing them to each little group as:

Gatsby   Mrs Buchanan, and Mr Buchanan – the polo player.

Tom   Oh, no, not me.

Gatsby   This is Mrs Buchanan – and Mr Buchanan, the polo player.

Daisy   I've never met so many celebrities.

Tom   I'd a little rather not be the polo player, you know.

Daisy   But you are.

Tom   I'd rather look at all these famous people in oblivion – say, do you mind if I eat with some people over there? A fellow's getting off some funny stuff.

Daisy   The fellow with the long blonde hair, you mean? Go ahead. And if you want to take down any phone numbers –

Nick   Meanwhile . . . Daisy and Gatsby danced.

A foxtrot.

The moon looked down from her cradle, and laughter rose high and drifted toward the ocean, and the party was unfurling as a dozen times before – But there was an unpleasantness in the air, an oppressiveness I hadn't felt before. And I realized – I was looking at it all through Daisy's eyes.

A partygoer comes up to **Daisy** *and says.*

Ross   The name's Ross, how d'you do? Is this your husband?

Daisy   Nick? Why, no –

Ross   We'll play golf together you and I, over at Westchester. What's your handicap?

Daisy   I'm afraid I don't have one –

A drunk woman called **Miss Baedeker** *comes on screaming and falls on* **Nick**, *who catches her.*

Nick   Whoa there, steady as she goes!

Ross   Miss Baedeker! Put a sock in it would you?

Miss Baedeker   Wha' you mean, put a sock in it?

Ross   When she's had five or six cocktails she starts screaming. You oughta leave it alone, Marie!

Miss Baedeker   You leave *me* alone!

Ross   And you oughta eat something. Come on!

Ross *and* **Miss Baedeker** *leave.*

Nick   Daisy was appalled by West Egg, this place that Broadway had begotten upon a Long Island fishing village. Her eyes scanned the crowd for some sign of her world reflected back to her, and saw none. When Tom emerged from the dark she nearly swooned with relief.

Tom   Who is this Gatsby, anyhow? Some big bootlegger?

Nick   Where'd you hear that?

Tom   A lot of these newly rich people are just big bootleggers, you know.

Nick   Not Gatsby.

Tom   Well, he certainly must have strained himself to get this menagerie together.

Daisy   They're more interesting than the people we know.

Tom   Interesting! That's a word for them.

Daisy   Lots of people come who haven't been invited, that's all – and he's too polite to object.

Tom   I'd like to know who he is and what he does. And I think I'll make a point of finding out. Here's the car.

Daisy   I can tell you right now. He owned a lot of drug-stores, he built them up himself –

Tom   Is that right?

Tom *leaves. Music* – Three O'Clock in the Morning.

Daisy   Good night, Nick.

Daisy *kisses* **Nick**, *then follows* **Tom**.

Gatsby *enters, stands with* **Nick** *watching the* **Buchanans** *leave in their car.*

Gatsby   She didn't like it.

Nick   Of course she did.

Gatsby   She didn't have a good time. I feel far away from her. It's hard to make her understand. She used to be able to understand –

Nick   He wanted nothing less than that Daisy should go to Tom and say: 'I never loved you'. And when she was free, they were to go back to Louisville and be married from her house – just as if it were five years ago.

Nick   I wouldn't ask too much of her. You can't repeat the past.

Gatsby   Can't repeat the past? Why of course you can!

Scene Ten

Nick *hands* **Jordan** *a glass of water.*

Nick   I'm all out of ice, sorry.

Jordan   At least it's wet. You know, I wish I could have seen them there. I can't believe I missed it.

Nick   Did you miss me?

Jordan   Oh, I missed everything! You, the cocktails –

Nick   That cinch of a putt on the eighteenth . . .

Jordan   Don't remind me!

The phone rings.

Nick   3289? Why hello, Daisy–

I know, isn't it? I was so hot on the train from the city I thought I'd –

Well, thank you, yes, I'd love to – matter of fact, Gatsby already called me about it –

All right. Till tomorrow at noon – Looking forward to it. Stay in the shade, won't you. Goodbye.

Jordan   Gatsby invited you already?

Nick   Yes.

Jordan   To Tom and Daisy's?

Nick   Yes.

Jordan   My.

Nick   Something's up.

Jordan   You don't say.

Nick   He fired all his servants, too.

Jordan   *All* of them?

Nick   He has these new people from New York, from his friend Wolfshiem.

Jordan   You're not serious.

Nick   Said he wanted people who wouldn't gossip.

Jordan   About Daisy being over there most afternoons.

Nick   Yes.

The newspaper says it's going to be even hotter tomorrow.

Jordan   Perfect. We'll just have to think about cold things.

Nick   That ought to do it.

Jordan   Cold thoughts.

Scene Eleven

Music – 'The Sheik of Araby'.

At the **Buchanans'** *house. As* **Nick** *enters, a* **Butler** *is serving drinks (with lots and lots of ice . . .).* **Gatsby** *is looking out of the window.*

Nick   Good afternoon, everybody.

Daisy *and* **Jordan** (*together*)   We can't move.

Gatsby (*meaning the drinks*)   They certainly look cool.

Daisy *laughs, she is nervous and excited.*

Nick   And Mr Thomas Buchanan, the polo player?

Tom's *voice is heard, off.* **Daisy** *gestures, 'that's him now, listen'.*

Tom   Well then I won't sell you the car at all! – I'm under no obligation, whatsoever –

Daisy (*cynically*)   Holding down the receiver.

Jordan   That's Tom's girl on the line, rumour has it.

Tom   I don't have to do anything about it – !

Nick   Actually it's a *bona fide* deal, I happen to know.

Tom   And as for your bothering me about it at lunch time, I won't stand that at all!

Tom *comes in.*

Mr Gatsby! I'm glad to see you, sir . . . Nick . . .

Daisy   We need another gin rickey. For Nick-ey.

Tom   All right.

Tom *goes off again.* **Daisy** *goes to* **Gatsby** *and kisses him.*

Daisy   You know I love you.

Jordan   There's a lady present, you know.

Daisy   You kiss Nick too.

Jordan   What a vulgar girl!

Daisy   I don't care!

Tom *comes back in, hands* **Nick** *his drink.*

Nick   Thanks.

Tom   They're saying pretty soon the earth's going to fall into the sun – or, wait a minute – it's just the opposite – the sun's getting colder every year. (*He approaches* **Gatsby**.) You're admiring the view.

Gatsby (*points*)   I'm right across the bay from you.

Tom   So you are.

Nick   After luncheon – taken in the funereal gloom of a dining room darkened against the heat – there was a nervous gaiety in the stifled air.

Daisy   What'll we do with ourselves this afternoon? And the day after that? And the next thirty years!

Jordan   Don't be morbid. Life starts all over again in the fall.

Daisy   But it's so hot! And everything's so confused. Let's all go to town! (*She turns to* **Gatsby**.) What do you say, Jay? Ah! You look so cool . . . You always look so cool . . .

Tom *breaking the spell.*

Tom   All right. I'm perfectly willing to go to town. Come on – we're all going to town.

They don't move . . .

Come ON. What's the matter, anyhow?

Daisy   All right, but do let's have fun about it. It's too hot to fuss.

Jordan   Will we take anything to drink?

Tom (*heading off*)   I'll get some whiskey, meet you at the garage.

Daisy   We'll go get ready.

Jordan   Let's.

Daisy *and* **Jordan** *leave.*

Gatsby (*to* **Nick**)   I can't say anything in his house, old sport.

Nick   There's something in her voice, something –

Gatsby   Her voice is full of money.

Gatsby *turns aside.*

Nick   That was it. I'd never understood before. That was her music, the jingle and cymbal of it –

Jordan, **Daisy**, **Tom** *and* **Gatsby** *join* **Nick**.

Tom   All right – (*To* **Gatsby**.) You take my coupé and let me drive your car to town.

Gatsby   I don't think there's much gas.

Tom   Well, if it runs out I can stop at a drug-store. You can buy anything at a drug-store nowadays. Come on, Daisy.

Daisy *evades his hand and moves to* **Gatsby**.

Daisy   You take Nick and Jordan. We'll follow in the coupé. Meet you at the Plaza?

Jordan   Mint juleps at the Plaza!

Daisy *walks off with* **Gatsby**. *She touches his hand.*

Tom   Did you see that?

Nick   See what?

Tom   You think I'm pretty dumb, don't you?

They get in the car and **Tom** *drives.*

I've made a small investigation of this fellow.

Jordan   Of Gatsby?

Tom   Yes, of Gatsby! Who else?

Jordan   And you found he was an Oxford man.

Tom   Like hell he is!

Jordan   If you're such a snob, why invite him to lunch?

Nick   We rode on in silence, irritable now with the heat and the lunchtime liquor. Then at the ash heaps I saw Dr T. J. Eckleburg's monstrous eyes looming out of the dust, and I remembered about the gas.

We should stop at this garage.

Tom   We've enough to get us to town.

Jordan   Well I for one don't want to get stalled out here in the desert.

Tom *slams on the brakes. They get out of the car.* **Wilson** *approaches.*

Tom   Let's have some gas! What do you think we stopped for – to admire the view?

Wilson   I'm sick, matter of fact.

Tom   You sounded well enough on the phone.

Wilson   I didn't mean to interrupt your lunch. But I need money pretty bad, so you see I wanted to know –

Tom   How do you like this nice yellow one? Want to buy it?

Wilson   Big chance. But I could make some money on the other.

Tom   What do you want money for, all of a sudden?

Wilson   I want to get away. Myrtle and me, we want to go West.

Tom   Your wife does?

Nick   At the mention of Mrs Wilson I saw her, at an upstairs window – staring at Jordan, eyes wide with jealous terror. She took her to be Tom's wife.

Wilson   She's been talking about it for years. Now she's going whether she wants to or not.

A sudden rush of car noise and the rasp of a horn as **Daisy** *and* **Gatsby** *drive past at speed.*

Tom   What do I owe you?

Wilson   I got wised up to something funny the last two days. That's why I want to get away.

Tom   What do I owe you?

Wilson   Dollar twenty.

Tom   I'll let you have that car tomorrow afternoon.

Wilson   I'm obliged to you, sir.

The three of them get back in the car and continue the drive to New York.

Nick   Tom was feeling the hot whips of panic. Until an hour ago his wife and his mistress were secure and inviolate. But now –

Jordan   I love New York on summer afternoons when everyone's away. There's something very sensuous about it–

Tom   'Sensuous.'

Jordan   Like it's overripe, do you know what I mean? It wants eating.

Scene Twelve

The Plaza Hotel. Music.

Jordan   It's stifling in here!

Daisy   We should have taken five bathrooms, an ice bath in each.

Nick   Yes!

Daisy   Open another window, somebody.

Jordan   There aren't any more.

Daisy   Let's telephone for an axe –

Tom   Forget about the heat, why don't you? You make it ten times worse by crabbing about it.

Gatsby   Why not let her alone, old sport?

Tom   That's a great expression of yours, isn't it? All this 'old sport' business. Where'd you pick that up? Oxford? I understand you're an Oxford man.

Gatsby   Not exactly.

Tom   Yes, I understand you went to Oxford.

Gatsby   I went there, yes.

From above or below the room comes the sound of Mendelssohn's Wedding March. *They stop and listen. Then the music stops abruptly –*

Nick   It must be the rehearsal.

Jordan   Imagine marrying anybody in this heat!

Daisy   I was married in the middle of June. Louisville in June! Somebody fainted . . . who was it . . .

Tom   Biloxi.

Daisy   Bill Biloxi!

Tom (*to* **Gatsby**)   He was at Harvard. Must have gone there about the time you went to Oxford.

Gatsby   I went there in 1919, for five months only. That's why I can't really call myself an Oxford man. It was an opportunity they gave to some of the officers after the Armistice. We could go to any of the universities in England or France.

Jordan   Come on, Tom. Have a mint julep.

Daisy   Have two – you won't seem so stupid to yourself.

Tom   I want to ask Mr Gatsby one more question.

Gatsby   Go on.

Tom   What kind of a row are you trying to cause in my house anyhow?

Daisy   He isn't causing a row. *You're* causing a row. Please have some self-control.

Tom   Self-control! I suppose the latest thing is to sit back and let Mr Nobody from Nowhere make love to your wife. Well if that's the idea you can count me out. I'm not very fashionable. I don't give big parties. These days I suppose you've got to make your house into a pigsty to have any friends –

Gatsby   I've got something to tell you, old sport.

Daisy   Please don't! Please let's all go home. Why don't we all go home?

Tom   I want to know what Mr Gatsby has to tell me.

Gatsby   Your wife doesn't love you. She's never loved you. She loves me.

Tom   You must be crazy!

Gatsby   She never loved you, do you hear? She only married you because I was poor and she was tired of waiting for me. It was a terrible mistake, but in her heart she never loved anyone except me!

Tom (*to* **Daisy**)   What's been going on?

Gatsby   I just told you – been going on for five years –

Tom   You've been seeing this fellow for five years?

Gatsby   We couldn't meet – but we loved each other all that time, old sport, and you didn't know. I used to laugh to think that you didn't know.

Tom   You're crazy! I'll be damned if you ever got within a mile of her unless you brought the groceries to the back door. Daisy loved me when she married me, and she loves me now.

Gatsby   No.

Tom   And I love her too. Oh, once in a while I go off on a spree and make a fool of myself, but I always come back, and in my heart I love her all the time.

Daisy   You're revolting. (*To* **Nick**.) You do know that's why we left Chicago. Because of a little 'spree'.

Gatsby   That's all over now. Just tell him the truth – you never loved him.

Daisy   I never loved him.

Tom   Not at Kapiolani?

Daisy   No.

Tom   Not that day I carried you down from the Punch Bowl to keep your shoes dry?

Daisy   Please don't. There, Jay! Oh, you want too much! I love you now – isn't that enough? I can't help what's past. I did love him once – but I loved you too.

Gatsby   Loved me *too*?

Tom   Even that's a lie! She didn't know you were alive.

Daisy   I can't say I never loved him. It wouldn't be true.

Tom   Of course not.

Daisy   As if it mattered to you.

Tom   Of course it matters to me. And I'm going to take better care of you from now on –

Gatsby   You don't understand.

Tom   Oh, I don't?

Gatsby   Daisy's leaving you.

Tom   Nonsense.

Daisy   I am, though.

Tom   She's not leaving me – certainly not for a common swindler who'd have to steal the ring he put on her finger!

Daisy   I can't stand this – please let's go –

Tom   I've made a little investigation into your affairs. He and this Meyer Wolfshiem bought up a lot of side-street drug-stores here and in Chicago and sold grain alcohol over the counter. I picked him for a bootlegger the first time I saw him and I wasn't far wrong!

Gatsby   I guess your friend Walter Chase wasn't too proud to come in on it.

Tom   And you left him in the lurch, didn't you? He went to jail because of you.

Gatsby   He came to us dead broke. He was very glad to pick up some money, old sport.

Tom   Don't you call me 'old sport'!

Daisy   *Please*, Tom! I can't stand this any more –

Tom   It's all right, Daisy. You two start on home, in Mr Gatsby's car. He won't annoy you. I think he realizes his presumptuous little flirtation is over.

Daisy *and* **Gatsby** *leave.*

Tom   One for the road? (*To* **Nick**.) What is it? You look like you saw a ghost.

Nick   I just remembered.

Jordan   What?

Nick   It's my birthday.

Tom   Happy birthday.

Jordan (*kisses* **Nick**)   Happy birthday.

Music – The 'Wedding March', loud.

Scene Thirteen

Wilson *is stalking* **Myrtle**. *He holds out the silver choker or necklace that* **Myrtle** *was wearing that night at the apartment.*

Wilson   You're gonna tell me straight out, or so help me God I'm gonna make you!

Myrtle   Make me? Oh Georgey.

Wilson   Where d'you get it from? Where?

Myrtle   Run along and play, Georgey boy.

Wilson   WHERE D'YOU GET IT FROM?

Myrtle   Temper, temper.

Wilson   Somebody bought it for you –

Myrtle   Yeah?

Wilson   And I want to know who!

Myrtle   You're ridiculous.

Wilson   Must be five hundred dollars' worth!

Myrtle   I found it, that's all.

Wilson   Oh, you found it?

He attacks her. She fights him off, with some success. Eventually she is cornered and in self-defence lands a heavy blow. He reels backwards.

Myrtle   That's right, Georgey! Beat your old lady!

Wilson   What you done to me, I oughta do it, and worse –

Myrtle   Knock her round like a big brave soldier boy!

George   I'll kill you, so help me!

He drags her towards the window and forces her to look outside.

Wilson   Think you can fool me, huh? Do you? Well maybe you can. But you can't fool God! He's watching you! He knows what you've been doing! He knows everything!

Myrtle *stops sharply. She can hear a car approaching.*

Wilson   Is it him?

Myrtle *breaks free, and rushes out the door – to her death. Cacophony of engine noise, emergency brakes, and the collision.*

Scene Fourteen

The same night, in East Egg, outside the **Buchanans**'.

Tom   Are you sure you won't come in for some supper?

Nick   If it's all the same, I'd just like to –

Tom   Let me call you that taxi, at least.

Nick   I'll wait by the gate.

Tom *goes in,* **Jordan** *comes out of the house.*

Jordan   You're not coming in?

Nick   Going home.

Jordan   It's only half past nine.

Nick   I'm thirty, now. I suppose this is how it is.

Jordan (*sadly*)   All right. Happy birthday.

Nick   G'night.

Jordan *goes,* **Nick** *sets off. He hears his name, and* **Gatsby** *steps out of the gloom.*

Nick   What are you doing?

Gatsby   Just standing here, old sport. Did you see any trouble on the road?

Nick   We did.

Gatsby   Was she killed?

Nick   Yes.

Gatsby   I told Daisy I thought so. She stood it pretty well. I got to West Egg by a side road and left the car in my garage. I don't think anybody saw us. Who was the woman?

Nick   Her name was Wilson, her husband owns the garage. Tom knows the man and spoke with him at the scene – and listen, Gatsby, there are witnesses to say it was a big yellow car and brand new –

Gatsby   I tried to take the wheel, but –

Nick   Daisy was driving?

Gatsby   I'll say I was, of course. The woman ran straight out in front of us – as if she thought we were somebody she knew, and wanted to speak to us – Daisy turned to avoid her but a car was coming fast the other way and she turned back in fright. I reached for the wheel and the second I touched it – I felt the shock.

Nick   She was ripped right open.

A pause.

Gatsby   I'm worried about Daisy. If he tries any brutality she's going to turn the light out and on again twice.

Nick   He won't touch her.

Gatsby   I don't trust him, old sport.

Nick   You wait here. I'll see if there's any kind of commotion.

I tiptoed my way round the side of the house till I saw a small rectangle of light – and there they were. Sitting at the kitchen table. Tom was talking intently. Once in a while Daisy looked up at him and nodded in agreement. They looked unhappy – and absolutely intimate. Anybody would have said they were conspiring together.

(*To* **Gatsby**.) It's all quiet up there.

Gatsby   Are you sure about that?

Nick   You know, it's pretty certain they'll trace the car. You ought to go away for a while, to Atlantic City, or up to Montreal –

Sound of a car horn.

Gatsby   I can't go away now, old sport. There's your taxi. Good night.

Nick *leaves.* **Gatsby** *keeps his vigil.*

Scene Fifteen

At **Wilson**'s *garage.* **Wilson** *is seated, hugging himself, rocking back and forth.*

Chorus   It's a shame
A goddamn shame
How long have you been married, George?
Ever had any children?
Come on there
How long you been married?
It's gotten late
Take some coffee

Some air
Some whiskey
Try and sleep a while
We'll sit with you if you want
Ever had any children?
You got a church you go to sometimes, George?
We could call it up
Get a priest for you
Times like this
You ought to have a church
Didn't you get married in a church?

Wilson   That was a long time ago.

Chorus   How long ago?

Wilson   My God. He murdered her.

Chorus   Who did?

George   He killed her.

Chorus   It was an accident, George.

Wilson   My God!

Couple of months ago she came home from the city and her
face was black and blue. How come, I says. Oh I had a little
'difference of opinion' with a girlfriend of Catherine's, she
says. Well, I knew she was lying to me then, but I let it go.
Then yesterday – this thing (*He shows the necklace.*) –

Chorus   You got a friend, George?

Somebody we can telephone for you.

Wilson   I told her, you might fool me but you can't fool
God! God sees everything! Then right that second, like a
thunderbolt! – that car. She ran out to him and he saw her in
the road and he murdered her. Him. And I have a way of
finding out who he is. I have a way.

Scene Sixteen

The terrace overlooking **Gatsby**'s *garden. It's early morning.*
Gatsby *and* **Nick** *are having coffee and smoking.*

Gatsby   Daisy was the first girl I ever really knew, of that
sort. There was a kind of mystery to her, and I was a little
overwhelmed, by her eyes on me and yes her wealth and her
freshly laundered clothes – and the fact that here I was, a
penniless Joe in the midst of all these riches and in the
presence of this young woman who was desired by so many
. . . I was drunk on it. I devoured it. Do you understand me?

Nick   You were in love with her.

Gatsby   I can't tell you how surprised I was. To find that I
really did love her. In the beginning it was a sort of exciting
game. I'd let her believe I was from her world, with a
comfortable family standing behind me – when all I really
had was the uniform. She thought I knew a lot because I
knew different things from her . . . So there I was, getting
deeper into love, further out of my depth, and all of a
sudden I didn't care.

She'd caught a cold and it had turned her voice all husky
and low, and – and we were sitting together on a wicker
settee on the porch. I leaned in to kiss her, and she
whispered something to me, and –

Nick   It's all right, you don't have to –

Gatsby   Her voice! God, her voice.

Two days later I was on the boat to Europe, and the war.
Where I did just fine. When the Armistice came I was frantic
to get home and find Daisy again, but I had to go where I
was sent and I was sent to Oxford. Meantime she had
resumed her social life –

Nick   And Tom came into view.

Gatsby   That's right, old sport. Mr Buchanan. I still think
she never loved him. She was over-excited this afternoon,

and he put things in a way that frightened her – that made it look as if I was some kind of cheap swindler. Of course she might have loved him just for a minute, when they were first married – and loved me more even then, do you see?

Nick   I do.

Pause.

Gatsby   They're draining the pool today. You know I haven't used it all summer?

Nick   A lot of other people did.

Gatsby   Care to swim?

Nick   I can't, I'm afraid. (*He looks at his watch.*) In fact – I have to run for my train. I'm expected.

Gatsby   Ah.

Nick   Thanks for breakfast. I'll call you up.

Gatsby   Do, old sport.

Nick   I'll call you this afternoon.

Gatsby   I suppose Daisy'll call too.

Nick   I suppose so.

They shake hands and say goodbye. As he goes . . .

Nick   They're a rotten crowd, Gatsby. You're worth the whole damn bunch put together.

Scene Seventeen

Gatsby *is in the pool. Music.*

Nick   No telephone call came from Daisy. I have the idea he knew it wouldn't, and no longer cared. He must have felt that he had lost the old warm world, paid a high price for living too long with a single dream. He must have looked up at an unfamiliar sky through frightening leaves and shivered to think what a grotesque thing is a rose . . . as an ashen figure, scarcely real, drifted toward him through the trees.

Wilson *comes and shoots* **Gatsby** *dead. Then* **Wilson** *goes off, and shoots himself.*

Scene Eighteen

Gatsby*'s body is laid out, photographed, covered and uncovered and photographed again . . .*

Nick   I remember the rest of that day, and that night, and the day after, only as an endless drill of police and photographers and newspaper men in and out of Gatsby's front door. A detective used the word 'madman' as he bent over Wilson's body – and in the whole sad circus to follow, Wilson's murderous actions were proclaimed and reduced to those of a man deranged by grief.

He goes to the phone, dials.

May I speak with Mrs Buchanan, please?

They leave an address?

Well do you have any idea when they might return?

I see.

He puts down the phone.

When they drew back the sheet the hundredth time I heard his protest in my brain:

Gatsby   Look here, old sport – you've got to try hard and get somebody for me. I can't go through this on my own.

Nick   I called Meyer Wolfshiem's office on Broadway but it was after five and nobody answered. I was half expecting him to shoulder his way through the door any minute, tears streaming down his face. The next morning, a letter came.

Wolfshiem   Dear Mr Carraway, this has been one of the great shocks of my life. I cannot come down as I am tied up but if there is anything I can do let me know by letter. I hardly know where I am when I hear about a thing like this and am completely knocked down and out.

Nick   A little grey man in a battered mackintosh arrived at the house and in a little grey voice he said:

Mr Gatz   I'm his father, Henry C. Gatz.

Nick   Mr Gatz –

Mr Gatz   I saw it in the Chicago newspaper. It was all in there, all of it.

Nick   I'm really so sorry.

Mr Gatz   Were you a friend of my boy's, Mr – ?

Nick   Carraway. Yes, I was. We were close friends. Would you like to see him?

Mr Gatz   I would, sir. He had a big future ahead, you know. He had a lot of brain power. He'd of helped build up this country.

Nick   I think that's true.

Mr Gatz *sighs and wipes his eyes.* **Nick** *pats him on the arm. Then* **Mr Gatz** *goes to the body.*

Klipspringer *comes in.*

Klipspringer   Hi there? Mr Carraway.

Nick   Klipspringer! I'm glad to see you, sir.

Klipspringer   Likewise.

Nick   You're rather early.

Klipspringer   I am? That's not like me!

Nick   The funeral's tomorrow, three o'clock. Actually – could you help me with some addresses? I want to send a wire to a few people –

Klipspringer   Happy to, but you know I really just came by for my tennis shoes. I'm sort of helpless without them. I've looked everywhere but the damned things are hiding from me –

Nick   Get out.

Klipspringer   Ah. I've offended you.

Nick   Get out!

Klipspringer (*as* **Nick** *throws him out*)   Would you have the butler send them on? The address is care of –

Nick   I was ashamed for Gatsby, a feeling that grew to a fever on the day of the funeral. The minister arrived and I asked him to wait for the cars that were surely making their way across the Island. But none came. Nobody came. At the graveside, Mr Gatz, the minister and I, wet to the skin. A couple of his staff came during the service. Then a car delivered up someone – it was the Owl-Eyed man from the library, that night three months before.

Owl-Eyes   I couldn't get to the house in time.

Nick   Neither could anybody else.

Owl-Eyes   My God. They used to go there by the hundreds! The poor son-of-a-bitch.

Nick   I tried to think of him, but he was already too far away. All I could remember was that Daisy hadn't sent a message. Not even a flower.

Scene Nineteen

Jordan *practises her swing,* **Nick** *comes and watches.*

Jordan   I so resent all these hours I have to spend 'practising'. But they simply can't be avoided. Like old boyfriends.

Nick   I was hoping we could part friends.

Jordan   You threw me over on the telephone, Mr Carraway. Nice move!

Nick   Jordan –

Jordan   Oh, I don't give a damn about you now. But it was a new experience for me, and I felt a little dizzy for a while. Do you remember a conversation we had once about driving? Cars, that is.

Nick   Not exactly.

Jordan   You said a bad driver was only safe until she met another bad driver. Well, I guess I did.

Nick   I never meant to hurt you.

Jordan   Goodbye, Mr Carraway.

Nick   Won't you shake my hand?

Jordan   Good luck out West. Drive safely.

Nick *leaves her swinging. At her last swing, an appreciative crowd noise and* **Jordan** *waves to the crowd before striding off.*

Scene Twenty

Nick   While I wound up my life in the East I spent the weekends in New York. I couldn't bear the sight of his house and the memory of the parties, the dazzle and gleam and ferocious music of them, all as dead as he. Then one October Saturday on Fifth Avenue –

Tom *comes striding through and they can't avoid each other.*

Tom   What's the matter, Nick? You look like you want to avoid me.

Nick   You know what I think of you.

Tom   You're crazy.

Nick   What did you say to Wilson that afternoon?

Tom *hesitates,* **Nick** *turns away.* **Tom** *grabs him.*

Tom   I told him the truth, that's all. He was mad enough to kill me if I hadn't told him who owned the car. His hand was on a revolver in his pocket the whole time. And what if I did tell him? That bastard had it coming. He threw dust into your eyes just like he did in Daisy's, but he was a tough one. He ran over Myrtle like you'd run over a dog. I went to give up her apartment – when I saw her dress on the bed I sat down and I cried like a baby. By God, I did.

Nick *holds out his hand. A curt shake.* **Tom** *goes.*

Nick   I couldn't forgive him, or like him. But I saw that what he had done was, to him, entirely justified. They were careless people, Tom and Daisy – they smashed things up, then retreated into their money, and let other people clean up the mess.

Scene Twenty-one

Nick   On my last night, with my trunk packed and my car sold to the grocer, I went over and looked at that huge incoherent failure of a house once more. The moon rose higher and I became aware of the old island here that flowered once for Dutch sailors' eyes – the new world. For a transitory, enchanted moment man must have held his breath in the presence of this continent, face to face for the last time in history with something commensurate to his capacity for wonder.

And I thought of Gatsby's wonder when he first picked out the green light at the end of Daisy's dock. He had come a long way to this blue lawn, his dream must have seemed so close he could hardly fail to grasp it . . . He did not know that it was already behind him, somewhere back in that vast obscurity. Gatsby believed in the green light, the future that year by year recedes before us. It eludes us, but no matter–

tomorrow we will run faster, stretch out our arms further, and one fine morning –

So we beat on, boats against the current, borne back ceaselessly into the past.

The End.

For a complete catalogue
of Bloomsbury Methuen Drama
titles write to:

Bloomsbury Methuen Drama
Bloomsbury Publishing Plc
50 Bedford Square
London WC1B 3DP

or you can visit our website at:
www.bloomsbury.com/drama

IMPR⟩V⟩⟩ ⟩O⟩ S:

Establishing and Integrating
Whole School Behaviour Policies

David Thompson and Sonia Sharp
with Mike Ellis and Derek Rose

David Fulton Publishers
London

David Fulton Publishers Ltd
2 Barbon Close, London WCIN 3JX

First published in Great Britain by
David Fulton Publishers 1994

Note: The right of David Thompson, Sonia Sharp, Mike Ellis and Derek Rose to be identified as the authors of this work has been asserted by them in accordance with the Copyright, Designs and Patents Act 1988.

Copyright © David Thompson and Sonia Sharp

British Library Cataloguing in Publication Data

A catalogue record for this book is available from the British Library

ISBN 1-85346-312-4

Typeset by Harrington & Co.
Printed in Great Britain by the Cromwell Press, Melksham